The Fight For Life

Taking It to the Streets

Catherine Davis

1st Edition

Printed in the United States of America

ISBN   1461109302

EAN   978-1461109303

To everything there is a season.
A time to every purpose under the heaven:
A time to love,
A time to hate,
A time of war
And a time of peace.

Ecclesiastes 3:1

Contents

Introduction: The Situation

In 1973 when *Roe v. Wade* was passed and abortion was legalized nationally, I remember having a discussion with my mother about it. In her mind, the black community would never be impacted by abortion, which she considered white woman foolishness. She rehearsed the black community's history of treasuring our children and, because of that history, she actually laughed out loud to think any black woman would kill her child in that way.

She so influenced my thinking that I believed blacks would never be swayed into believing abortion was a right that superseded the right to life. While I knew some black women would individually make the decision to abort—I myself would be among them—it did not sink in that abortion would become so common that black abortion would disproportionally lead the nation. In a strange way, I somehow divided the issue in my brain.

I believed my mother, that the history of having our children sold was in our genes, and our genes would prevail. She was right that there was a time in the black community when it would have been unconscionable for a black woman to even consider killing her children for being unwanted or inconvenient. Despite being raped by slave masters or KKK members, black women bore their children with dignity—a dignity that surpassed the daily obstacles of race and ethnicity placed before them. Many black women suffered the indignity of being considered the mammy of a child who appeared to be white when it was indeed her own child. These women kept and raised their children proudly, despite massive legal and social injustice against them.

There was a similar staunch attitude during the Jim Crow era. My memories of being black in America were of strong black men and women who defied the odds and raised their children differently, to help them succeed when society had set them up to fail. Blacks suffered the indignity of being shuffled aside when whites passed, and when they were made to sit in the backs of buses. They had to fight, and even bleed, to make a new way for their children to live. In fact, their children were their hope and motivation for civil equality.

So never did I suspect that even though recent generations of blacks have had no Jim Crow or slavery, that we would embrace the idea of controlling our birthrate through abortion.

The plain fact is that abortion is on the rise all over America. Since 1973, there have been *55 million* abortions in this country. That means we have killed approximately 17% of our current population, almost 1 out of every 5 babies. And abortion is growing in strength and popularity today, as government healthcare gets behind it. The pro-abortion lobby has systematically fought every roadblock that pro-life legislators created to set it back: parental notification, informed consent, the woman's right to know, a required ultrasound, the 24-hour waiting period, and fetal pain legislation that bans abortion on a baby 20 weeks or older. I live in Georgia, which is a state that has enacted most, if not all, of these laws. Despite these valiant efforts, the numbers of abortions has not declined significantly. Abortion is in the hearts and minds of people now. We're familiar with it, numb to it. It has become a right that women cling to, as a sign that they are free, and this "right" will not easily be given up.

But what's even worse is that the black community has been targeted by the abortion lobby, drawn into its killing dens, and borne the brunt of the abortionist's handiwork. They have been made to laud its results and carry the flag for the agenda which is depopulating it, cheerfully believing it is the way to salvation, freedom, economic prosperity. The reality is heart-wrenching, and no-one wants to talk about it. This is why this book has been written.

Let's start with some basic facts. Did you know that over *18,870,000 blacks* have been aborted since 1973? This number continues to rise at the rate of *1450 per day*. Instead of the streets, alleys, woods, and trees of Selma, Atlanta, or Birmingham, the womb is now the place of terror for the black race. Even though blacks make up only 12-13% of the American population, 37% of the nation's abortions are on black women. Does that seem right to you? Had these babies not died at the abortionist's hands, blacks would actually be 19% of the population today. In fact, our population level has hovered around the same levels since 1930. I am going to argue that this is unnatural—designed intentionally by those who first thought up family planning and abortion services, and furthered by those who still have a similar agenda.

In some communities, such as New York City, the toll is even more devastating. Recent numbers suggest that black babies are now being aborted in that city at a higher rate than those who are born alive. In 2010, for every 1000 black babies born alive in that city, 1448 were aborted.[1] In other words, New York is being depopulated of blacks. Not surprisingly, New York City is where the very first birth control clinic was established, and abortion offered. It is the quintessential picture of where the abortion industry would like to take the black community in every city across the nation.

They very well may be getting their way already. In Georgia, where I live, the number of total abortions has increased or remained at the same level each year, while black abortions are not only the majority of abortions but are also going up. Georgia currently has an abortion rate of approximately 30,000 babies per year, which is horrific in and of itself. But between 2005 and 2008, much more than half of those—58%—were black abortions. In 2009 and 2010, it was 59%. Since 1994, there have been more than 255,000 black babies taken out of Georgia's population! That's just in seventeen years, just in one state!

These horrific numbers beg for a new legislative strategy that blazes a new, radical trail—not just follows an incremental path. What we're witnessing today is genocide, and it has to be stopped immediately.

How? I believe unborn babies should be provided the same measure of protection that blacks were afforded through the Civil Rights Act of 1964. While some may balk at the comparison of the abortion industry to Jim Crow, abortion is murdering millions of blacks and has become a dominant cultural and government institution just like segregation was. It is why the rest of this book will center around my work trying to craft a similar bill, which

[1] http://www.nyc.gov/html/doh/downloads/pdf/vs/2009sum.pdf

would extend similar anti-discrimination measures to babies in the womb. It was through laws, through the Supreme Court, that the door opened for human life, black life, to be devalued for the first time in the Dred Scott case. Then again in *Plessy v. Ferguson.* This third time, through *Roe v. Wade*, we can't let them get away with it again. America's citizens aren't sub-human property whether black or white, born or unborn. I intend to elevate life to its rightful place by defining the right to life as paramount through antidiscrimination law.

To those who can't understand why abortion should be seen as a scourge rather than right, you have to realize that more black babies die by abortion than the seven leading causes of death in the black community combined.[2] The horrific history of slavery and Jim Crow has not overridden the abortion rhetoric which has been hurled daily at the black community. The abortion industry has succeeded in overriding our heritage and writing a new grotesque one for our future.

Not many are brave enough to hear this story though. Are you? I want to challenge you to open your ears to the truths I will tell you. Come with me on this journey to see for yourself what has been going on behind closed doors. The pro-abortion lobby certainly doesn't want its dirty little secrets exposed. They do not want America to focus on the fact that the abortion industry is marketing its services to black women every day in school-based clinics with their billboard campaigns and other advertisements. They do not want you to notice how abortion clinics target black, urban communities completely disproportionately and make their money off minorities, immigrants, and the poor. And they definitely don't want the statistics we have just shared to get out. Then you might start questioning the dogma they have been feeding you.

The abortion culture wants America to remain blind to the fact that there is an outside influence drawing so many black women into the abortion dens. No-one wants to talk about how race is a confirmed factor in the abortion industry's agenda and growth. They want us to think the results are just incidental. Abortion's popularity rests on the assumption that there is no

---

[2] http://cnsnews.com/news/article/abortion-kills-more-black-americans-seven-leading-causes-death-combined-says-cdc-data

evidence that black children—or any children—are unusually endangered. Anyone who thinks otherwise is kooky and "stepping on the rights" of women everywhere. Rather than investigate abortion providers and their practices, so the truth can be plainly seen, abortion defenders hide under a storm of rhetoric which includes pointing the finger at any whistleblower for being racist, sexist, and intolerant.

This includes me, a black woman. One of the more perplexing things I have encountered is the refusal of blacks to recognize the truth about abortion. Granted, I have probably read way too many melodramatic novels, but in my heart I thought that once the abortion industry was exposed, there would be an uprising all across the nation to stop it. I had visualized blacks from every stripe and persuasion coming together to demand that the tyranny of abortion be eradicated. I am still reeling from the realization that abortion has become so deeply rooted in our culture that black women are unwilling to condemn it. I am dismayed that anyone can ignore the history of racism and discrimination in order to participate in abortion's killing fields.

So this book is about confronting this difficult issue head-on. Clearly, the stakes have changed in the fight for rights. At stake are not only civil rights, but human rights and the lives of millions of babies, little human beings that abortionists don't want America to think about. Also at stake is the very legacy of the African-American community. Without babies there is no African-American community, there is no heritage, there is no lineage, and there is no life.

Chapter 1: The Call to Fight

When I was growing up, if a person wanted to start a fight, he would draw a line in the sand and dare his opponent to step across it. Or he would place a stick on his shoulder and tell his opponent to knock it off. If the opponent were brave enough, he would cross the line or knock the stick off and the fight would start. In the 1970s, America's abortion industry put a stick on its shoulder and drew a line in the sand, daring Americans to stop their population control agenda. To this day, we haven't.

Thirty-nine years ago, times were different. Our culture promoted children as gifts from God, and most Americans did not believe women would embrace the act of abortion, especially in communities of color. However, within two years of abortion being legalized, abortionists started taking more than a million lives every year. What started as a brawl between pro-life and pro-abortion forces quickly grew into a siege, a Holocaust that has extinguished the lives of more than *fifty five million* babies in the womb.

In response, a resistance movement began. Organizations such as National Right to Life mobilized to slow the advances of the newly sanctioned abortion industry. Care Net and Heartbeat International developed well thought-out strategies and began working to rescue one baby, one mother at a time. Legislative action was initiated, and all around the country incremental measures were launched in efforts to stop the advances abortion was making and change the minds of abortion-minded women. Civil disobedience groups such as Operation Rescue sprang into action. Many of these groups had a Christian foundation. In 2007, 40 Days for Life carried the banner of reaching abortion-minded women through prayer and fasting in front of abortion mills.

While some of these skirmishes slowed the tidal wave of abortion rights, they did not stop the tsunami. America was on the fast track to using abortion as a primary means of birth control, and more sinisterly, of population control, mostly in communities of color. What was once abhorrent became accepted, and now cherished. Abortionists became less careful about cloaking their message as they felt increasingly secure that women would always demand this newfound right to end life in the womb. Now abortion has been twisted into a tool for women's freedom and health. To decry it is to deny a woman her basic rights.

In this environment, there is a need to fight differently from the way pro-lifers have traditionally fought—a need to enlist and deploy new recruits onto the battlefield. Some of the battle-scarred and weary warriors are simply worn out, having held the line for so long that they are stretched thin. They should be allowed a moment to rest. But the nature of the battle has changed significantly too, and old warriors need to be replaced with new recruits who better understand the art of war. New soldiers in the fight must have great strength, courage, and a will to face down those who want America to believe abortion is good and should be provided freely. Those who know how to street fight should be placed on the front line. It is time for the pro-life surge!

It is critical that those who are squeamish, fearful, or lack the will to fight, stay home. Those who would rather pontificate, theorize, or debate the merits of abortion on demand also need not enter this war. Those whose homes are not in order for whatever reason, also need to stay home. This type of distracted warrior can be a detriment to the whole army. If the enlistee promotes division on any level, or criticizes the efforts of others to end abortion, immediately send them home - they don't know how to keep rank. The fight for unborn babies requires the measure of unity Jesus spoke of in John 17:11—"Now I am departing from the world; they are staying in this world, but I am coming to you. Holy Father, you have given me your name; now protect them by the power of your name so that *they will be united just as we are*" (emphasis mine).

Like Gideon, we must separate those who might hinder the fight from those who are battle ready (Judges 7:1-8). Our troops must be capable of carrying the weight of each battle lest we all go down in defeat. The fearful will hurt us. The self-absorbed will hurt us. Only those who are alert, who can recognize the battleground and understand war, need come. Because fighting abortion is like a street fight, and street fighting *requires* a united front. Everyone in the fight must be able to trust those who are with them to get their back. If there is no covering, if there is betrayal in the ranks, if those fighting with you don't know how to keep rank, victory is in jeopardy and the warriors are at risk of perishing.

I know this from personal experience. When I was a young girl, my mom used to say, "Girls don't fight." That is, until I came home one too many times with a bloody nose, hair pulled out, or torn clothing. Finally, she released me to defend myself. From that day forward, I fought boys or girls—it did not matter. The fights continued all the way to high school, although by then they were not quite so frequent because I had gained a reputation.

The way it worked was, I grew up on the west side of Stamford, Connecticut in a housing project called "the Village." Now the Villagers did not play when it came to fighting. We were seasoned street fighters, having fought each other over the years. Sometimes the Village would fight groups from one of the other projects on the west side. Other times, we would fight groups from the east side or south end. When that happened, we fought as one. Even though we may have scrapped among ourselves the day before, we became one against the enemy, and it was the Village against whomever. Other times, youth from a different city would challenge us from Stamford. Once again, divisions evaporated and it was Stamford versus whichever city was foolish enough to want to fight us.

The measure of unity we demonstrated with one another in the Village sometimes extended to the whole state of Connecticut when we were challenged by youth from another state like New York. It was us against them. And when blacks as a whole were challenged, again all schisms and divisions disappeared. It became us against whoever "they" were – the larger white society, the government, whomever. Divisions evaporated when it came to fighting for our causes.

I emphasize unity here because unity is such an important factor in any fight, and we don't have enough in the fight against abortion. The fight for unborn lives is really no different from my fights for the Village. The pro-life movement has gained a lot of ground but is sadly crippled by division. Even within the side which trumpets the pro-life cause—the Republican Party—there are those who put on the uniform but don't fight with us. Some are deceived by opponents into being soft or compromising. Some don't actually believe in the cause. Others are more insidiously working against us from the inside, intentionally betraying us.

The fight for the unborn requires more than this. It requires the kind of fighting skills I acquired in my youth, and the kind of passion and stalwart unity each side fought with. I still move the boundaries when I see the battle lines of attack, whether in the state of Georgia or the nation as a whole. It is us against them – pro-life vs. pro-abortion. We are in an epic national battle for the lives of babies and the soul of the nation.

As an unsaved youth, there were certain behaviors I would not tolerate, so whoever had the temerity to engage me in one of those situations would get slapped, kicked, punched or whatever. But then I got saved. I finally conceded that I was not doing a great job of directing my life and asked Jesus to come into my heart and take control. After my salvation experience, I thought my fighting days were over because Kingdom believers couldn't go around slapping or punching people like I had grown accustomed to doing.

Imagine my surprise as I began to read and study the Bible to find out that believers actually *do* fight! Granted it is not a physical fight, but there is definitely a war spiritually. We are told in Ephesians 6:12 that "...we are not fighting against flesh-and-blood enemies, but against evil rulers and authorities of the unseen world, against mighty powers in this dark world, and against evil spirits in the heavenly places."Even though I am not punching and slapping human beings as I fight for life, I am fighting nonetheless. I am engaging spiritual weapons against spiritual forces which ravage innocent people.

Furthermore, as believers, we are called to pick up the pro-life cause. One night while reading the Bible, I came across the Scripture in Matthew 2:18—"A cry was heard in Ramah, weeping and great mourning. Rachel weeps for her children, refusing to be comforted, for they are dead." As I read that Scripture, I felt a tug in my heart to cry for the children of America who were being aborted. I knew that I was to fight for babies *and* for the soul of America. Why the soul of America? The Bible is clear that the shedding of innocent blood is one of the seven things God hates (Proverbs 6:6-19). A nation that sheds innocent blood on demand will be—must be—held accountable. Our hearts cannot remain hardened against our children or the nation will die the same ignoble death of those nations that came before us that killed their children as a routine practice.

Next, I began learning about modern abortion's roots in America, and how it was wrapped up in a movement called eugenics—a progressive, racist ideology. I read *Grand Illusions: the Legacy of Planned Parenthood* by George Grant, which helped me understand that the nation's largest family planning organization was waging war specifically against the black community, and the poor, and others whom the elite considered unfit. I committed right then and there to change this intolerable situation.

But what could I do? How does a believer in Jesus Christ fight in a war like this one? The first step I took was to volunteer with two organizations: The Network of Politically Active Christian Women, and Virginia Right to Life. Through both these groups, I had more speaking engagements than I could handle. I relished these opportunities to call attention to the devastation of abortion, hoping I was making a difference. Those days were great. I frequently spoke to legislators, educators, and political groups. I went into churches, community centers, and neighborhood programs, delivering a pro-family, pro-life message.

I spoke at a number of political events on behalf of candidates who styled themselves as pro-life, racing from one engagement to another, and bringing our message to any and all who would listen. I was able to interact with some of Virginia's most prominent citizens and politicians such as George Allen, Virginia's newly elected Governor, and Kay Cole James, Virginia's Secretary of Health and Human Services. Despite our successes in this political arena, the stream of women into abortion clinics was not abated. It became crystal clear that more was needed than successfully speaking on behalf of politicians. In my mind, the fight should be moved to the greatest corridor of political power in the world, Washington DC.

At this point, J. C. Watts, a black Republican and rarity in the nation's capital, had just been elected to serve in the Congress. I thought of joining his team specifically to reach out to the black community. I wanted to encourage black participation in conservative politics as well as expose the political agenda of the family planning industry to control the birth rates of those they considered inferior. I actually arranged to meet the good Congressman in hopes of bringing that dream to life.

But God had a different path laid out for me. My pastor, Bishop Wellington Boone, began talking about moving to Georgia. Even though I was happy for him and those who had committed to the move, I was not one of the families volunteering to go with him. Believe me when I tell you, I am no groupie. There were seventy-four families who committed to move, and I had no desire to be family number seventy-five. As I was wishing him well, however, Bishop Boone said something to me that caused me to wonder if I should consider Georgia rather than Washington. His simple question was, "If I am your Pastor, why aren't you moving with me to Georgia?" As I said, I am no groupie and had no desire to go to Georgia. But my decision wasn't to be based on those factors.

Bishop's question drove me into my prayer closet. I had to be sure that my plans for my life lined up with God's plans for my life. So I began to pray, asking God whether I was to join the others and move further south rather than north. The very first night that I prayed, I randomly opened my Bible and read Jeremiah 3:15, "And I will give you shepherds after my own heart, who will guide you with knowledge and understanding." Well now, I had never seen that particular passage before and began to wonder if God was indeed telling me to become family seventy-five. So as not to presume such thoughts, I shamelessly bargained with God. Like Gideon, I put out a fleece and asked Him for impossible confirmations that I was to move to Georgia.

Here is how the fleece was answered. When George Allen was elected as Virginia's Governor, the state's General Assembly was majority Democrat. At the beginning of Allen's administration, almost every bill that was presented split along party lines and, up until that point, none of the Republican-sponsored bills had passed. It was in this environment that the Governor began discussing his desire to downsize state government. His plan was to offer state workers, of which I was one, one week's pay for every year they had been with the state if they would resign. The General Assembly, as was expected, said no. But they agreed with the concept of saving money through downsizing. So Allen offered *two* weeks' pay for every year the employee had been with the state, plus health and life insurance for a year, *and* a $5000 lump sum payment to anyone who volunteered to be downsized.

I thought that plan had a snowball's chance in hell of passing, so I prayed and asked God to allow that bill to pass unanimously if my children and I were supposed to be family number seventy-five. God answered that prayer exactly as I had prayed it, and on August 6, 1995, I packed hearth and home and moved to Georgia!

Now that I was in Georgia, what was I to do? I started a journey where I collected facts, identified strategies, and honed my skills. Georgia became my boot camp and the place where I still know the victory will come.

Action Steps

1. **Self-Assess.** All too frequently we become passionate on a matter and believe we are to fight, fight, and fight, only to give up. Make sure you are in the fight to win it, no matter how long it takes.

2. **Educate yourself.** Abortion is a moral issue shrouded in an aura of darkness. Delve into the history of abortion and how it came to be legal in this nation.

3. **Read your Bible.** Some battles are won in the Spirit and we cannot fight in the Spirit if we do not know the Spirit.

4. **Volunteer.** Find a pro-life organization and give them some of your time and/or money! Help an organization reach abortion-minded women.

5. **Pray** God will end the scourge of abortion in America.

Chapter 2: Abortion's Racist Foundations

Abortion has been wrapped up in a progressive, racist agenda from its very inception. Today, the biggest abortion provider is Planned Parenthood, which is government-funded to control the population of poor regions both nationally and internationally. This means massive extermination for communities of color all over the world. This trajectory was originally developed in 1914 by Planned Parenthood's founder, Margaret Sanger, who was disturbed about urban black poverty.

Like many social elites of her day, Margaret Sanger was concerned that America was developing a large black underclass which posed a threat to the health and economic stability of America. She thought birth control was the answer and set about trying to create an organization to bring down the black birth rate. Based in New York City, she started a hub where she hired black medical personnel and black ministers to evangelize black mothers into using contraception. She and some wealthy entrepreneurs such as Clarence Gamble (of Proctor & Gamble) were on a quest to find the best birth control for the "uneducated masses."[3] Once found, they thought, it could become part of a public health program, enshrined in law and funded by tax dollars. Then "Negroes...the great problem of the South" would be fixed![4]

By the 1930s, this was officially called "the Negro Project." You see, Margaret Sanger and her supporters were *eugenicists*, which means they thought undesirable traits—such as darker skin color, lower intelligence—could be weeded out of the human population through controlling and minimizing reproduction among people with those traits. This idea came directly from evolutionary theory, which took as its founding premise that human races were

1http://www.nyu.edu/projects/sanger/secure/newsletter/articles/bc_or_race_control.html

[4] Ibid.

18

different species, uncreated by God, and inherently unequal. The full title of Darwin's pioneering book on evolution was *The Origin of the Species by Means of Natural Selection: the Preservation of the* **Favored Races** *in the Struggle for Life.*[5] Though we hail it today as the treatise which reoriented all of modern science, it had racist notions hopelessly enmeshed with it.

In this book and subsequent ones, Darwin developed the idea that black people were an intermediate species and would most likely extinct itself. Well, eugenicists applied these ungodly ideas to society to speed this along. It is no surprise that the father of eugenics, Francis Galton, was Darwin's own cousin. Galton wasted no time applying evolutionary theory to society and quickly became the proponent of a program of selective breeding that encouraged the most successful individuals to have many children while sterilizing the weak, handicapped, and mentally ill. Without guidance, eugenicists said, the less desirables would outnumber the more desirables, and then where would the world be? The poorer and less desirable you were, the more you needed to be limited in how much you would reproduce. This is context modern birth control was developed in. Margaret Sanger realized that sterilization wasn't going to weed enough bad traits out and began Planned Parenthood to start extincting the poor and black communities even faster. Freed from Christian morality, Galton and Sanger saw themselves as doing good for society, just hastening evolution along.

But how to get this message across? A poor minority community wouldn't accept a message coming solely from white scientists and social planners. It only made sense that black ministers should be paid to preach birth control from the pulpit. Sanger herself told Clarence Gamble, "We do not want word to go out that we want to exterminate the Negro population, and the minister is the man who can straighten out that idea if it ever occurs to any of their more rebellious members."[6]

Birth control could be construed as "extermination?" Well yes, if you were overheard like Sanger was, reciting such racist propaganda as:

[5] The Origin of the Species by Means of Natural Selection: the Preservation of the Favored Races in the Struggle for Life, London: John Murray, Albemarle Street, 1859.
[6] http://asteria.fivecolleges.edu/findaids/sophiasmith/mnsss43_main.html

- "Eugenic sterilization is an urgent need ... We must prevent multiplication of this bad stock."[7]

- "Eugenics is ... the most adequate and thorough avenue to the solution of racial, political, and social problems."[8]

- "The campaign for birth control is not merely of eugenic value, but is practically identical with the final aims of eugenics."[9]

- "Give dysgenic groups [people with 'bad genes'] in our population their choice of segregation or [compulsory] sterilization."[10]

These statements were just the tip of the iceberg of those that revealed Sanger's institutionalized racism. Notably, she only ever talked about "Negroes" even though there were many other ethnicities in America at that time including Jews, Asians, and Eastern Europeans. Her definition of "dysgenics" and "weeds"[11] were laced with the common pejoratives of the black race in her day. This is important because Planned Parenthood defenders today avow that their organization has nothing to do with racism. If you bring up anything Margaret Sanger actually said, they will attempt to minimize her eugenic moorings, or spin them as progressive and compassionate to the plight of black poverty. But roots run deep. She was in fact well connected to racially motivated eugenics societies that sprang up across America in the early 1900s, and so were those on her team.

This is the context in which abortion was developed. It was not developed as a tool of personal choice, individual freedom, or sexual liberation—it was a killing machine developed on purpose to solve the "problem" of the poor urban black community. Birth control was just the first step—Planned Parenthood was originally called the "Birth Control Federation of America." Abortion, however, was a much better solution because it could be used once the "mistake" of conception had occurred. If undesirables forgot, didn't like, or couldn't acquire birth control beforehand, there was

[7] Margaret Sanger, April 1933 Birth Control Review

[8] Margaret Sanger. "The Eugenic Value of Birth Control Propaganda." Birth Control Review, October 1921, page 5

[9] Ibid.

[10] Margaret Sanger, April 1932 Birth Control Review.

[11] http://www.dianedew.com/sanger.htm

still a nine-month window to still get the results social planners wanted.

It is important to dwell on this point because society has been indoctrinated to believe that contraception and abortion are tools for individual rights, women's rights, and civil rights. Take them away and we are back in slavery, poverty, and the confines of domesticity, they say. But birth control was developed for the black community to extinguish itself—most birth control methods were actually field-tested on poor black women![12] And abortion took over the role of birth control as birth control proved to be slow and ineffective in changing the statistics.

Eugenicist elites knew what would happen as abortion was increasingly practiced by all but especially the black community—that's what they wanted in the first place! The slow racial genocide, the targeting, the unbalanced black abortion statistics—all were part of the plan from the beginning. Today we are confronted with the fact that no matter the rhetoric, abortion is doing what it was designed to do.

If this sounds particularly Nazi-like, it is. Eugenics actually preceded Nazi Germany and fueled the fire of the Holocaust. By the early 1900s, all kinds of Western elites, not just those in America, were enthralled with the idea of limiting the birth rates of those deemed inferior. A number of progressive "philanthropists," well-respected, joined together to fund and promote eugenics as the basis for population control. Backers such as the Gambles, Rockefellers, Carnegies, and Harrimans sought to control the birth rate of those considered to be "weeds and misfits," as Margaret Sanger put it. In fact, it was a Rockefeller-funded eugenics program that gave Josef Mengele (Nazi Germany's angel of death) his start![13]

While this agenda of purifying the human population quickly led to ruthless ethnic cleansing in Germany, in America it was cloaked in more fashionable, progressive clothing. Birth control and abortion could be packaged in careful language which made it seem logical and compassionate. To be sure, there was a radically racist agenda. Radical eugenicists suggested sterilization,

[12] http://nyu.edu/projects/sanger/secure/newsletter/articles/bc_or_race_control.html

[13] Eugenics and the Nazis, The California Collection, San Francisco Chronicle. Sunday, 2November 9, 2003, page D-1

segregation, and marriage restriction among anyone deemed undesirable, and America experimented with those for awhile. Indiana was the first state to enact a compulsory sterilization program in 1907,[14] and 33 other states followed suit. Together, they sterilized over 60,000 men and women, many without their consent or knowledge, and a considerable number being poor, uneducated black women.[15]

Most states also had laws barring interracial marriage or affairs well into the 1960s. By the 1950s, half of the states in America passed miscegenation laws barring marriages between different ethnicities.[16]

Then more insidious programs were implemented for those who were considered "dysgenics" and therefore expendable. Deadly and deteriorating diseases were purposely introduced into unsuspecting groups such as those in the Tuskegee Syphilis Study and the Puerto Rico Cancer Study where patients were deliberately injected with syphilis and cancer cells as part of a scientific discovery experiment.[17] Of course, Nazis were convicted of such crimes following World War II, but in America, they flew largely under the radar.

Eugenics was fashionable throughout the early 1900s—the wave of the future, ensuring the human population would be fit for ages to come. But the more radical elements of eugenics lost face with the condemnation of Nazism after World War II. Abortion needed to find a new way to survive so people wouldn't see it for the racist social planning tool it was.

Through the 60s, abortion was able to reinvent itself with new packaging. At the forefront of everyone's minds was bucking the system. In the case of civil rights, this was a good thing—the only way America would get out of the maze of Jim Crow. In the case of the counterculture, however, this was a bad thing. Suddenly

[14] http://www.uvm.edu/~lkaelber/eugenics/IN/IN.html

[15] Human Experiments: A Chronology of Human Research by Vera Hassner Sharav , retrieved July 5, 2009 from http://www.ahrp.org/history/chronology. php

[16] Wiker, Benjamin D and Donald De Marco. Architects of the Culture of Death. Ignatius Press, 2004. page 302.

[17] Black, Edwin. War Against the Weak, Eugenics and America's Campaign to Create a Master Race Four Walls, Eight Windows:2003, page 131-135.

morality was up for grabs, and youth culture latched onto sex, drugs, and rock and roll...and abortion.

Feminism and environmentalism were two ideologies which helped recast abortion in a positive light, after its dark eugenicist past. They changed the American consciousness about abortion from being a dirty, underground occurrence to a celebrated tool of progress. Feminism said women needed freedom from rules about sex. They ought to be able to indulge in their sexual pleasures as much as men, unattached, unemotional, and free from the consequences—including babies. Abortion made this dream possible. It became the cornerstone of women's sexual freedom—complete security that even if birth control were to fail, young girls wouldn't be "burdened with a baby," as President Obama put it in his recent public defense of abortion. Gone were the days of shame concerning premarital sex. American women should have choice!

Environmentalism also became a pillar of abortion defense because it became fashionable through the 60s and 70s to believe that mankind's existence was damaging the earth. There was a huge overpopulation panic in the late 60s, as environmental scientists predicted physical and economic apocalypse if mankind didn't get control of its reproduction rate immediately—especially in poor, underdeveloped areas. Population control was therefore fashionable, compassionate. Abortion was officially sanctioned by university professors, environmental activists, and global government workers. Sure it flew in the face of religious tradition, but what was that when the world was at stake? Some leading lights even went so far as to say it was Christian attitudes about marriage, sex, and children which were damaging the planet in the first place! They were what was causing all this poverty we now had to clean up. Slowly, mainstream America's attitude towards abortion started changing.

Abortion's advance was both a root and a fruit of this value change. Taking the helm of Planned Parenthood from Margaret Sanger in 1962, Dr. Alan Guttmacher expanded the tools of the eugenics movement to include abortion at will. Historically, abortion had been restricted to cases where a "continued pregnancy would endanger a pregnant woman's life or endanger her health..."[18] But Guttmacher convinced the powers that be, that this endangerment should include the "more general and indefinite threat... including especially her psychological heath."[19] In other words, a woman should be allowed to get an abortion for basically no reason at all. Any perceived discomfort could be interpreted to mean her "psychological health" was threatened.

Over time, and through his personal practice in New York, Dr. Guttmacher was able to erase the line between physical health and psychological health when it came to abortion. When Roe v. Wade was decided in 1973, Guttmacher's definition of psychological health was progressive and popular. So the Court's companion case to Roe, Doe v. Bolton, expanded the definition of "health" to fit that which Guttmacher had been practicing.

This opened the door to late-term abortion, partial-birth abortion, and all the horrific practices we have today. Abortion on demand at any stage of the pregnancy has become the rule rather than the exception because under the umbrella of "women's health," an unborn baby can be aborted for the simplest of reasons at any point—anxiety over weight gain, for example, or the fact that the baby is the undesired gender. Under Guttenmacher's definition, there could be no legal restrictions on abortion.

This was both permitted by radical feminism and pushed it further. Indoctrinating America to believe that Planned Parenthood was a "trusted reproductive healthcare provider," Guttmacher's diabolical scheme to "allow for unrestricted copulation without fear of pregnancy"[20] found its way into the corridors of mainstream America which then went through a sexual awakening with dire consequences: over 55 million abortions since 1973, about 20 million of which have been performed on black women. Of course Guttmacher knew where things were headed when he became involved in shaping abortion policy in the first place. He was not only Planned Parenthood director, but he was the Vice President of the American Eugenics

[18] U.S. Supreme Court. DOE v. BOLTON 410 U.S. 179 (1973).
http://caselaw.lp.findlaw.com/cgi-bin/getcase.pl?court=us&vol=410&invol=179. Accessed 8/22/12.
[19] Nelson, Jennifer. Women of Color and the Reproductive Rights Movement. NYU Press: 2003. page 85.
[20] Ibid.

Society. He believed abortion was a tool for racial population control just as much as Sanger had.

After Roe v. Wade passed, the issue of life moved to the political front burner. More and more politicians began to campaign as pro-life or pro-abortion. Slowly but surely, new concepts were tested that helped change the language of the pro-abortion community. As society accepted abortion as a viable tool for population control, abortionists introduced the notion that abortion is a measure of redress for economic concerns. People were told it was no longer unconscionable to think of aborting a baby if the parent or parents were facing economic hardships.

In fact, it was a compassionate choice. Think of the life a child would have had without enough money, and the resources which were then freed up to go to those who were living. This economic calculus replaced the traditional view that children were a blessing who would continue the parents' legacy. No upwardly mobile person could value children if they were essentially a financial drain. Neither could the poor. Babies were just another mouth to feed, bringing them down.

This new message was how the abortion rhetoric made it into the black community. It was preached to the rooftops that abortion would lift people out of poverty—pretty much what Margaret Sanger had said, but with a more progressive spin. Abortion was not evil, they said. It was a moral good! Only a backward, mean-spirited society would allow its poorest people to have many babies, keeping them stuck in poverty. This is how Planned Parenthood was allowed to continue its eugenicist attack on urban, black communities while convincing those communities that it was a good idea. More abortions for more black women? It seemed to be a win-win strategy.

Sadly, the black community itself started accepting this lame proposition. By 1973, when more than 30 states had established eugenics boards, the culture was ripe for convincing women who had been civilly dead for so long that the playing field could be leveled by taking control of their bodies. Blacks, who had legally had been denied rights, were fed this dogma as a solution to the treatment they had received at the hands of America's slave and Jim Crow cultures. By taking control of their bodies through abortion, black and white women were told they were cementing a right and finding a voice they had not had until Roe v. Wade. But in actuality, the old eugenics agenda was still there. It was at this time that Frederick Osborne, the President of the American Eugenics Society, said abortion and birth control were the leading eugenic advances of the 20th century.[21] Who really cared how it was sold, as long as it was advanced?

Then respected leaders in the black community began to parrot the pro-abortion argument that abortion is a viable option for lifting blacks out of poverty. I first heard this idea posited by Loretta Ross, Founder and National Coordinator of SisterSong, in a February of 2010 New York Times interview. Ross said, "Controlling our fertility was part of our uplift out of poverty strategy, and it still works."[22] It is ironic that no one questions this nonsensical statement, and instead accepts it as fact. Very few in the mainstream media, black media, or other outlets challenged this outrageous statement, nor did they examine the poverty rates to see if there was any validity to it.

Fast forward to today, and SisterSong has actually become its own contemporary version of Margaret Sanger's Negro Project. The first time I heard the myth that black women actually asked Sanger to put her clinics in black neighborhoods was in a New York Times article having been introduced by SisterSong. Loretta Ross stated, "The reason we have so many Planned Parenthoods in the black community is because leaders in the 20's and 30's asked for them."[23] Could she have done the eugenicist's dirty work for them any better?

This is a great example of the boldness of the pro-abortion community. They put out information that has no basis in fact, and the media accepts it as if it is 100% accurate and correct. They repeat this rhetoric in story after story, never checking the facts in the same way they check statements from those who are pro-life. On the contrary, if the pro-life community makes any assertions, demands are made for documentation of the statements and full

[21] Frederick Osborn, Transcript, Oral History Interview (July 10, 1974), Columbia University, New York, 1977, p.7

[22] New York Times, Anti-Abortion Ads Split Atlanta, February 6, 2010 , Page A9

[23] http://www.nytimes.com/2010/02/27/us/27race.html

citations must be given. There is not one iota of information that could be found to support this assertion by SisterSong. Not one.

There are numerous articles, books, speeches and other documents, however, that suggest exactly the opposite is true. Combing through the history books, I found information that suggested the black woman was too close to the time when her children could legally be taken from her arms and sold, to have supported the notion of limiting her fertility by introducing a chemical or other device into her body. The memory of slavery was too dominant in her psyche, and the idea of not having children or not participating in the increase of blacks in this nation was abhorrent. If there were women back in the 20's and 30's that felt they wanted birth control, they were a minority so small that there is no documentation of their thoughts—at least none that I could find.

But so begins the descent into the mind of the feminist who supports abortion. I tell you, that mind is a maze of dogmatic ideology and unfailing ardor. It's a mindset that transforms the pro-abortion woman into a super hero fighting to protect women's rights. America's feminists did their job well. For thirty-nine years they dehumanized the child, slowly stripping away the pinnacles of the Christian faith that tells us we are made in the image of God. They redefined words so that the baby is no longer considered a person. Instead, they encourage expectant mothers to believe the baby is a "problem: that can be disposed of" at the discretion of the woman.

Actually, SisterSong was one of the agencies that attended the May 10th Congressional Black Caucus's (CBC) and Pro-choice Caucus briefing. It was SisterSong's strategic points that were distributed at the meeting. It was SisterSong that built the dossier that talked about me and my work, inaccurately stating that I want to shame black women. Truth is definitely not their banner.

I soon found out that this group was at the center of the messaging for pro-abortion groups around the nation. Partially funded by Planned Parenthood, SisterSong provides talking points, rallies women in protest, and coordinates anti-life activities around the country. I had discovered several of their articles while completing my research on abortion in America, and honestly dismissed them because they appeared to be chock full of misleading and inaccurate information. Much of the writings were nothing more than propaganda created to bring a measure of acceptability to induced terminations of pregnancy. It was not until much later in the fight that I realized each article they wrote actually tightened the stitches of the tapestry the abortion rights industry was weaving. Each article was strategically written and designed to cement their doctrine in the minds of the public, making it all the more difficult to undo. Margaret Sanger would have been proud.

Despite the fact that the information on eugenics is openly available and widespread, these women's collectives give it no consideration when promoting choice. They see conservatives' fight for life as being racist against people of color. In their minds it is "evil, white conservatives" who want to control the birth rate of blacks, not Planned Parenthood and the others whose ideology has historically supported population control of dysgenics.

It is ironic that their ideology of reproductive justice calls for no interference with a woman's right to choose, even though that choice is having a severe impact on blacks. I had at one time believed that when I presented the facts of eugenics and abortion to the black community, that organizations like SisterSong would immediately join in to stop the racial targeting. This has not been the case. In fact, because of organizations like SisterSong, the indoctrination of abortion has penetrated so deeply into the black community that there is confusion between the conflicting "rights" – the child's right to life versus the woman's right to choose.

They have worked to refocus the public's attention toward the woman's right to choose without any regard to the consequence of that choice on the child, on blacks, or on the nation. They don't realize that fighting for their right to kill an innocent human being is a perversion of liberty. They think they have a right to abortion that others are trying to take away.

In actuality, their right is to have their own heritage flourish without being unfairly targeted by the abortion industry. But because of the knee-jerk reaction to fight for any right being taken away, they can't hear the facts about abortion's impact on their own community. In order to save face, they choose to organize against us. In doing so, they reinforce the notion that the baby in the womb is nothing more than tissue to be wiped away for the mother's (or father's) convenience. They act as if the child can gain the right to life independent of the mother.

The point is, the eugenicist's line of thinking not only motivated the original abortion industry back in the time of Sanger, it still motivates it today. It has gone through a number of packaging changes, but the basic rationale that Sanger and the first population control enthusiasts believed in is still in full force: stopping reproduction will enrich yourself, your community, and ultimately the whole earth.

This had to be sold to the black community which had a natural and historical commitment to its young. But it was done successfully through the promise of civil rights and an end to poverty. To this date, abortion has helped further neither of those things. After four decades of legalized rampant experiment, it has only furthered racial division, encouraged eugenicist thinking, and decimated the black community. It has turned the black community upon itself, and parents upon their children. Those who should be the sacred guarders of their heritage are now fooled into tearing it down with their own hands.

Action Steps

1. **Research.** Find out your legislator's stand on abortion. Lobby him or her to be proactive, and take the lead in ending abortion in your state.

2. **Determine** whether your state had a eugenics board. If it did, find out when it was dissolved. Also determine if any of its board members, or relatives of board members, are still active in public policy.

3. **Educate.** Take steps to educate those in your sphere of influence about eugenics and family planning.

4. **Encourage.** Urge others to support the pro-life organizations which fight the eugenic forces in the nation. Support can be in the form of volunteering or donations.

5. **Pray.** Pray that God will restore the sense of the sanctity of life and end the scourge of abortion in America.

Chapter 3: Eugenics in Politics

I was soon going to find out for myself that the old eugenics mentality which had worked its way up through Sanger, Guttmacher, and the Courts was indeed still alive and well today, in public policy. In 2008, I received a call from the Executive Director of the Network of Politically Active Christians asking me to lobby for the passage of the Human Life Amendment. This was the bill that Georgia Right to Life was offering during that legislative session which would have amended the Georgia constitution to define the human as a person from the earliest biological beginning to death thereby protecting the baby from the threat of abortion by invoking the 14th Amendment.

Specifically, I was asked to lobby the Black Caucus and other Democrats while the Georgia Right to Life lobbyist, Mike Griffin, was to lobby the Republicans. I thought this assignment was going to be easy. I figured that once the black elected officials learned of the adverse impact that abortion was having on blacks, they would naturally be for the amendment. Because of the racially destructive impact of abortion, I even thought they would lobby their fellow Democrats and bring them to the side of the unborn baby. So "Ebony and Ivory" (Mike Griffin and I–as a joke we always called him "Ebony" and me "Ivory") began our assignment with relish, eager to win the day.

Oh, how naïve and blind I was! I am sure I did not effectively lobby even one black legislator because I found myself tripping and stumbling over the roadblocks that so-called pro-life Republicans were throwing in front of us. I quickly learned that not all Republicans were as pro-life as they led us and their constituents to believe. Many did not ascribe to the official Republican Party platform that says: "Faithful to the first guarantee of the Declaration of Independence, we assert the inherent dignity and sanctity of all human life and affirm that the unborn child has a fundamental individual right to life which cannot be infringed.[24]"

a 2008 Republican Party Platform http://www.gop.com/2008Platform/

So we ended up trying to convince many Republicans just to adhere to their own platform. In the meantime, it was ironically reported that there were enough Democrats in favor of the pro-life amendment to pass it, if only the Republicans would bring it to the floor. Go figure!

The most obstinate stumbling block was the Republican Speaker of the House, Glenn Richardson. Within weeks (the General Assembly in Georgia is only in session forty legislative days each year so things happen rather quickly), we began to hear that the Speaker was a racially motivated pro-choicer along the lines of eugenics pioneers Margaret Sanger, Rockefellers, and Carnegies.

At that time, I absolutely believed the legislature was the way to go in order to change the status quo. Margaret Sanger had made her first forays to establish her birth control clinics through the legislature and they rejected her efforts. It was at this point that she turned to the courts and walked the slow but methodical road to legalizing birth control despite America's Comstock Laws that forbade it. Finally, after thirty or more years of efforts, she found allies on the Supreme Court and in the 1965 *Griswold v. Connecticut* case, the anti-birth control laws were summarily struck down. This one act, I believe, opened the door to the sexual revolution and all that has followed in the war on life. It also opened the door to more insidious population control measures that had long been the goal of America's population control enthusiasts.

Others besides Sanger had tried to use the legislature for population control. One example was found in the 1969 Memorandum to Bernard Nerelson, former president of the Population Council. The Jaffe memo (Frederick S. Jaffe was Vice-President of Planned Parenthood-World Population) proposed measures to reduce the overall birth rate in the United States. Encouraging homosexuality, compulsory liberal sex education of children, and a restructuring of the family were but a few steps outlined in support of their goal. Unfortunately, there was not a corresponding proposal to defeat these ideas, and over time they took root in the fabric of America's culture.

The acceptance of these ideas had consequences in Georgia, just as they did throughout the nation. We found it common that legislators would evaluate pro-life legislative requests based on costs to the taxpayer and economic impact. Reports were that when the Georgia Legislature introduced the Women's Right to Know Bill in 2006, Glenn Richardson, the Republican Speaker of the House said that passing that piece of legislation would result in Georgia being "**overrun with black babies**." Another legislator claimed the Speaker had justified Planned Parenthood funding in 2007 because if it were halted, it would "**result in the birth of more black babies**" and, "**more black babies would be born and on the dole.**" The eugenics mindset was now controlling the legislature of Georgia.

Needless to say, there was a compelling need to determine if these statements were true. Alveda King, niece of Dr. Martin Luther King, Jr. and daughter of Reverend A. D. King, and I were invited by the Speaker's Chief of Staff to meet with Speaker Richardson to bring clarity to the matter. Of course we accepted the invitation and on February 12, 2008, she and I met with him. We left dumbfounded, discouraged, and angry about what transpired in that meeting.

The Speaker, while stating he did not say the words quoted above, said he "may have said something like that." And no matter how many times Alveda and I asked him what the "something like that" was, or even to explain how race came up in the discussion at all, he refused to answer. Instead, he just redirected the conversation to the statistically accurate facts concerning black high school dropouts (over 50%) in Georgia, or the abortion rate of black women in Georgia (58% at that time). He consistently attacked the legislators whom he believed had misquoted him, indicating they were at war with one another. And he insisted that he-could not understand why that particular legislator waited two years to say anything.

In other words, at no time did the Speaker clarify his position on black births in Georgia or his feelings about blacks in general. Instead, he deflected our questions by attacking those he believed had told us about their conversations. A black Representative later told me the Speaker even went so far as to approach some of the members of the Black Caucus the next morning, characterizing me as a bitter black female who was upset that he did not support my Congressional race in 2006. At that time he told me he could not support me because he did not want the "**black voters in DeKalb County**" to turn out – the good old southern strategy that Republicans have employed since the sixties.

Not too long after, the Speaker boldly proclaimed in a public meeting at the Cobb County Republican Party breakfast, that the Human Life Amendment would not make it out of Committee. He then had the bill assigned to the Judicial Subcommittee, whose Chair told us it was the "committee from hell." As he predicted, the committee from hell did the Speaker's bidding and the Human Life Amendment was killed. This blatant power play allowed many of the so-called pro-life legislators in the House to hide their discomfort and beliefs about the question of whether a baby in utero is a person. It was appalling and disheartening to watch so many men abandon their professed principles and sought-after endorsement from Georgia Right to Life in the face of the tyrannical control the Speaker exercised.

I watched men and women turn away from every campaign promise they had made to fight for life, simply for fear of losing…I am not sure what. Perhaps they agreed with the eugenics agenda of controlling black birth rates—not through lynching or other KKK initiatives, or Jim Crow, but through abortion. Perhaps they feared losing their chairmanships, or office location, or…well, I am still not sure why so many of them caved in the face of this tyranny. What I did learn was that the blind trust of Republicans with which I began my lobbying efforts was foolhardy and I needed to spend more time identifying the true "enemies" of life rather than assuming all those with an "R" behind their names, or those with the endorsement of Georgia Right to Life, were truly pro-life.

On a personal note, since the time these events occurred, Glenn Richardson has stepped down from his position as Speaker. I have spoken with him and find him to be a contrite, humble person today who has accepted Jesus as his guide. I applaud Glenn for the changes he has succeeded in making in his life.

But others still harbor these eugenicist attitudes, even those who seem to be the most progressive. I was appalled in July 2009, when Supreme Court Justice Ruth Bader Ginsburg confirmed the agenda of abortionists as one of population control. She said straight out: "Frankly, I had thought that at the time *Roe* was decided, there was concern about population growth, and particularly growth in populations that we don't want to have too many of."[25] Now what "populations" [26]was she referring to, other than the one Margaret Sanger consistently referred to - Negroes? I honestly believed this admission would provoke our people to put the final nail in the coffin of abortion. I assumed her comment would break open the doors of deception surrounding the abortion industry and even the politicians who most endorse it. But there was no outcry—not from progressives, not from the Church, or the black community—from no-one!

Eugenicist attitudes are still harbored in Planned Parenthood, the voice of progressivism. It has never deviated from that plan launched so long ago. They have consistently stuck to recruiting black ministers and leaders, and have consistently put a black face in the forefront of their marketing and legislative efforts. Documents have even been uncovered which lend evidence to the abortion industry's targeting of the black community. These documents include the 2008 tax filing of Planned Parenthood, which explicitly admits their purpose is population control.[26] They also include the transition plan given to President-elect Obama, and numerous blogs, articles, and position papers written by pro-abortion advocates.

One such article was written by Lisa H. Harris, Assistant Professor in Obstetrics & Gynecology and Women's Studies at Ann Arbor, Michigan. As she urged the pushing of the boundaries in second trimester abortions beyond 20 weeks, she defined being African-American as a risk factor for late term abortions.[27] Talk about targeting and offensive, this one had me shaking my head for a long time.

In 2011, a colleague of mine was invited to Georgia State to make a presentation about his campaigns on behalf of blacks being targeted by the abortion industry. Shortly after he had

[25]http://www.nytimes.com/2009/07/12/magazine/12ginsburgt.html?pagewanted=all

[26]
http://www.plannedparenthood.org/files/PPFA/PPFA_FY09_Form_990_Copy_for_Public_Inspection.PDF

[27]LH Harris / Reproductive Health Matters 2008;16(31 Supplement): page 79

arrived, a group of young, mostly white women showed up chanting, "Georgia State students trust black women." As my colleague attempted to allow them to air their concerns, it quickly became clear that their only motive was to shut him down. Having been trained, I believe by the Trust Black Women arm of SisterSong, these young women said the most horrific things to the black women in attendance. One young lady said that when a black woman chooses abortion, "...she is choosing the lesser of two evils." Another said, that "black women have abortions to be a better mother." And then adding insult to injury, they said black women need the government to give them birth control because they are poor! These kinds of lies are parroted across social media sites like YouTube, Twitter, and Facebook.

There are many more examples where abortionists target and discriminate against the black community, betraying their eugenicist mindset. One North Carolina abortionist stated his motivation very clearly when he encouraged pro-life activists to "adopt one of those ugly black babies". He encouraged them to "take them off the taxpayer money."[28] How was this attitude any different from the eugenicist attitude of Glenn Richardson?

The truth is, the practice of abortion is the most deadly terroristic tool that has been employed against blacks to date. Our elected officials have become bystanders to genocide on America's shores. They have led from behind by pushing black women toward the abortion chambers. America is experiencing the greatest mass atrocity in the world. And so many of the victims have no voice in it except mine and yours.

---

[28] http://www.youtube.com/watch?feature=player_embedded&v=f01PFcBicQY#!

Action Steps

1. **Identify** your state and federal elected officials and their positions on the right to life.

2. **Talk** about their position to your friends and neighbors who are voters.

3. **Enlist** their support of officials and candidates who will show leadership on the matter of the right to life.

4. **Pray** that God will end the scourge of abortion here in America.

Chapter 4: Engaging the Battle

I must admit that I entered the battle more naïve than I thought I was. While I knew to count the cost, I did not scout out the battleground because I thought I understood it. And as a result, I did not fully grasp that the battle was being fought on more than one front. Because there were several battle fronts, it sometimes meant fighting those who were considered allies, such as the legislators we battled in the Georgia House. But it also meant fighting those whose livelihood rested on communicating the abortion message to communities of color.

At this point in the fight, I had violated rule number one – Know Thy Enemy. I was not fully aware of all the opponents to life I had to face. I knew about Planned Parenthood, NARAL, NOW, the National Abortion Federation, and other anti-life groups. Their names periodically surfaced in the media or I had gathered the intelligence through the books and articles I was reading. What I did not realize at that point was that these organizations were implementing the modern day Negro Project by employing blacks to make their arguments for them, constantly deflecting the issue toward a civil rights ideology.

The first time I heard of SisterSong, the Women of Color Reproductive Justice Collective, I thought it was an organization that would fight to make sure abortion did not discriminate against women of color. I actually wrote them a letter encouraging them to meet with me and other black pro-lifers so we could join forces to fight against the elitist agenda that seeks to control the black birth rate. Instead of fighting alongside us, these women made it clear that they actually opposed us. Despite our impassioned plea and explanation of the facts about the detrimental effect of abortion on communities of color, they continue today to promote abortion. They are only interested in seeing that the government doesn't "interfere" with the so-called right of choice.

Shortly after being introduced to SisterSong, I learned about the Religious Coalition for Reproductive Choice (RCRC). The men and women in this organization claim they are "fostering a public dialogue about sexuality and reproduction embodying the values of liberation and wholeness that infuse the world's religions." In other words, they support abortion by actively speaking against those they characterize as the Religious Right. Their past president, Carlton Veazey, was compensated with more than $200,000 for about five hours of work per week, according to the group's tax filings.[29]

I then met face to face with Vanessa Cullen, Planned Parenthood's $240,000 Vice President of medical affairs. Ms. Cullen is an African-American so she is the person Planned Parenthood uses to reach other blacks. Yes, promoting the abortion industry's dogma can be quite lucrative for some blacks who are committed to the agenda, no matter how deadly it is to the very people they purport to help. Ms. Cullen flies from community to community to promote Planned Parenthood's population control agenda.

These combatants, along with "pro-life" legislators like those we faced in Georgia, made advances which enabled them to defeat our efforts. Needless to say, it was disconcerting to lose these battles so early in the fight. No one likes to lose. Yet, those losses became teachable moments and because of them, we grew wiser. We learned that adversity comes from unexpected sources. This created a new sense of urgency that we must get our message out directly to grassroots America. Such a tactic would circumvent those leaders who are being paid to spin the issue and those who are using it for leverage to get elected.

Before beginning the lobbying effort on behalf of NPAC, I was a human resource manager at a Fortune 40 telecommunications company. I was in my tenth year when they decided they no longer needed my services and I officially joined the ranks of the unemployed. I was laid off with a severance package that allowed me a year to regroup and reposition myself.

About midway through the severance, I began to search for a new position. Throughout my search, I prayed I would find a

29   http://www.guidestar.org/FinDocuments/2010/521/213/2010-521213972-07473571-9.pdf

position in something other than human resources. I had had my fill of crafting win-win resolutions to manager and employee complaints. I was no longer interested in hiring employees, firing employees, evaluating employees, or dealing with all the other issues that come with managing a staff and supplying sound HR advice. I began to pray about jobs that would allow me to impact the issues that are near and dear to my heart – a position that would make a difference for the family.

The door that was opened through the Network of Politically Active Christians revived a part of me that had been buried for some time. It was exciting to participate in activities that would make a difference, such as the protests that black pro-life leaders held in Washington, D. C. in 2008. Many of us were surprised to learn that, in spite of a ban which specifically prohibits providing Title X money to organizations that include abortion as a method of family planning, Planned Parenthood was receiving close to *one million dollars a day* in taxpayer revenues through Title X.[30]

When we found out, we partnered with Kristen Hawkins and Students for Life, lending our voices to the campaign to defund Planned Parenthood. A number of black pastors, ministry and community leaders, and pro-life organizations converged on the 16th Street Planned Parenthood site to protest the organization's receipt of taxpayer dollars. We were particularly incensed because Planned Parenthood is the leading provider of abortions in America, and is therefore a contributor to the disproportionate number of blacks receiving abortions. Taxpayer money in their hands meant dead black babies.

At the same time we were rallying to defund Planned Parenthood, new information came into our hands that was revealed through an undercover investigation conducted by Lila Rose's organization called Live Action, out of California. The operation produced recordings of phone conversations between a person posing as a donor to Planned Parenthood, and the organization's representative. Tape after tape revealed Planned Parenthood's willingness to accept donations specifically designated by the donor to terminate the life of a black child. No matter how vile the donor became, each Planned Parenthood agent agreed to accept the donation offered without so much as even an

[30] http://www.plannedparenthood.org/about-us/annual-report-4661.htm

objection to the language used. This was the spark that ignited a flame of indignation. Leaders such as Dr. Alveda King, of Priests for Life, Pastor Clenard Childress, of LEARN Northeast, Day Gardner, of National Black Pro-Life Union, Pastor Stephen Broden from Fair Park Bible Church in Dallas, Texas, and many others stood as one voice demanding that Congress investigate the organization's willingness to take monies to target black babies.

As Dr. Lily Epps prepared to speak, she remembered that it was in this very facility she was told her soon-to-be-aborted child was a problem. Her chilling "mad" black woman speech struck a chord that is still ringing in the ears of many of those who were in attendance. As each of us processed the overt racism she spoke of, and meditated on the fact that taxpayer funds were enabling this atrocious behavior, a sense of unity and commitment arose among us. This concord of sentiment birthed the National Black Pro-life Coalition. Those demonstrations also initiated national legislation.

Congressman Trent Franks of Arizona made a commitment to those present that day, that he would sponsor legislation which would address race as a factor in abortion. Shortly thereafter, he sponsored the Prenatal Nondiscrimination Act (PrNDA), which would restrict race and gender selection abortions, as well as coercion of women to obtain a race or gender selection abortion. The bill was designed to hold the doctors accountable for performing an abortion they know is race or gender based. With the introduction of that bill, there was a shift in the fight, and suddenly the discussion at a national level was beginning to focus on abortion as it relates to the black community.

A month after that event, national black pro-life leaders such as Bishop Harry Jackson of High Impact Leadership Coalition, Rev. Arnold Culbreath of Protecting Black Life, and Dean Nelson of the Network of Politically Active Christians, lent their influence to the growing movement and joined their voices with more than 100 others in front of the RNC and DNC to demand that Congressional candidates and Representatives return any contributions received from Planned Parenthood and other abortion providers. We made the appeal to black candidates and white, Democrats and Republicans, because candidates and elected officials who accept funds from Planned Parenthood are agreeing to speak for that organization and its eugenics agenda. We found this to be unconscionable in light of the tragic impact abortion is having on blacks.

Increasing numbers of black leaders were coming on board to challenge the status quo, and many joined us in Cincinnati, Ohio where a large contingent of black pro-life leaders urged the NAACP to not only recognize the genocidal impact of abortion on the black community, but to make ending abortion a part of their legislative agenda across the nation. It was heartbreaking to see the response of the NAACP leadership and the lengths they went to, to avoid the message of life. They refused to acknowledge these conservative leaders, instead making attempts to keep their delegates from seeing our messages of life.

Within thirty days of leaving Ohio, Dr. Johnny Hunter of LEARN and Pastor Stephen Broden urged the group to unite and become a coalition devoted to the sanctity of life. A diverse group of national black leaders met in Atlanta, Georgia and later in Fayetteville, North Carolina to develop a strategic plan that outlined specific steps leaders should and could take in their communities. The Strategic Plan for the African American Pro-Life Movement was crafted to provide a framework for informing, educating, and activating the black community. The plan provided action steps that would not only demonstrate solidarity among black leaders, but would ensure our efforts never migrated toward fighting each other. Instead it would take the street fight attitude of keeping focused on the enemy—abortion, the number one killer of black Americans.

Once drafted, the plan was introduced to black conservative leaders from across the country. I was excited to have been able to connect with these insightful leaders. I realized each of those participating would be a force that would initiate change in the paradigm of abortion at will in America.

Action Steps

1. **Determine** if the NAACP in your area supports or opposes abortion.

2. **Provide** the NAACP membership with information about the tragic impact of abortion on the black community.

3. **Pray** that God will end the scourge of abortion here in America.

Chapter 5: Fight Like a Man

Before I became a Christian, when I fought, I never fought like a girl. You know—eyes closed, arms flailing about, hoping to hit something. Fighting like that would have ensured my defeat as well as injury to some part of my body. I always fought with my eyes open in a deliberate fashion, picking and choosing my punches. I chose when to throw the punch and I calculated where to throw it, i.e. the chest, arms, face, etc.

Usually I was the one to throw the first punch because I understood the first punch would define the fight. If I thought you wanted to fight me, I would simply walk up to you and hit you where I knew it would hurt the most. Guys, you know where I mean, and ladies, it usually took just one punch to the face and the fight was usually over in my favor! Doing this always ensured I could throw a second punch, and if you were still standing or had not run away, it gave me time to run!

Now that I am a Christian, I know I cannot walk up to people and hit them. I cannot reach into my purse and pull out my Vaseline and grease my face, hands and arms, as many of those we fought against did—you know, so that if a punch landed it would slide off, or it would make it difficult for your opponent to hold you. But I knew I had to have a strategy, an idea of what to do before I entered the fight. So how do you actually fight a war you believe the Lord is calling you to? Since I couldn't punch someone into stopping abortion, I turned to the only Source that could tell me how to fight. I turned to God and began to ask Him, in prayer, for specifics on what I should do.

The first thing He led me to do was purchase and read Sun Tzu's *The Art of War*. I know that sounds strange, even borderline crazy to some people, but I did. I just felt led to read it, to understand how warriors think. And as I read this book (written, some say, in the 6th century B.C), I actually began to glean nuggets of wisdom that I could use to help me fight the battle before me.

At first I thought a lot of what I was reading was quite demonic. I mean to think that all war is won by deception!?! What was that? But I kept reading to see where it would take me.

Upon finishing *The Art of War*, I pulled out my Bible to see if I saw any resemblances between what I had read and how the Scriptures said the great men of the Bible fought their wars. It was a "wow" moment for me because as I read, I began to see real examples of the principles Sun Tzu expounded. I placed the Bible and *The Art of War* side by side and actually began to take notes.

Stories of Joshua, Gideon, David, and Paul encouraged me to fight with the weapons that are "not carnal, but mighty through God to the pulling down of strongholds" (2 Cor. 10:4). Comparing *The Art of War* with the Bible was really a lesson on how to fight God's way rather than with my fists. After finishing this study, I started ordering books, articles, studies and other materials about abortion in America. My reading list grew as I sought the answer to the question, "How did we get here?" As I delved deeper into abortion in America, I saw a pattern developing, and that pattern was chilling.

Then I knew I had to employ the Biblical model to combat the demonic pattern revealed in my study of abortion. When Joshua, Moses, David and others were fighting, they asked the Lord if they should fight and if so, which tribe they should send. Each time that they failed to ask God what they should do, there were serious consequences, such as when Joshua sent the men to fight the little town of Ai (Joshua 8) and they were beaten soundly. Joshua also made a pact with the Gibeonites (Joshua 9) and again failed to ask God whether he should. As a result, after Saul broke the covenant Joshua had made with them, Israel had a price to pay years later through a famine and the lives of seven of Saul's sons. In Judges 20, the Israelites did ask God if they should fight, but because of their sin, they were still beaten back two times before God gave them the winning strategy.

From this study, I understood that I had to ask in prayer for direction concerning each step I was to take in this war. I also realized there would be times that God would send me into a battle that I would not win outright, but should be fought nonetheless. I understood I would have to come back again and again, sometimes taking a few hits in order to break down decades of deception surrounding abortion.

Let me stop here to reassure you that I am not in any way diminishing or downplaying the role that big pro-life players have played in keeping this issue alive in America's courts and legislatures. There are many heroes of the movement who have fought battle after battle with the National Organization of Women, National Abortion Rights League, and Planned Parenthood among others. These courageous warriors have not shrunk back from the fight, but have run to the front lines again and again.

Yet, I believe there is a measure of street fighting that must be done in order to significantly impact abortion. A street fighter never goes into a fight uninformed. Most good fighters gather as much intelligence about their opponents and about winning strategies as possible, in order to increase their chance of winning. One thing they have learned is that you never go into a fight while high off a recent victory. Doing so clouds your ability to make good judgments about the conflict at hand. Seasoned fighters also know they must be armed with a mindset to expect the unexpected.

Words are one of the greatest weapons used in this fight for life, on both sides. It is the abortion industry, however, that has taken the greatest care to use words to persuade and create the illusion that they are nurturers, champions, and friends of women. They have echoed the Supreme Court, influencing the culture to believe abortion is a right granted under the Constitution and, as such, is a practice that should never be restricted. If any state attempts to restrict abortion in any way, the pro-abortion forces turn out, marching and chanting in opposition to whatever law is being proposed. Today the big pull is to fund abortions with taxpayer money so they can be provided for free, as part of routine healthcare. If you are against this, you are part of the "war on women." Well there is a war, but it is not against women.

Abortionists have always framed the debate in terms that will draw blacks and other minorities into their web, encouraging them to fight *for* the very tool being used to decrease their birth rates—and therefore, their representation. In framing the debate, pro-abortion groups manage to redefine words and create imagery that encourages society to think of abortion as a normal procedure within the reproductive arena. The message they have crafted is specific to the two groups which are most starved for rights in this country – blacks and women. Every weapon they have deployed is aimed towards convincing women to override their consciences, and the religious teaching that babies are human beings and blessings from God.

The war over words is a central front. They have convinced women that the alternative to carrying a child to term is "intervention" while it is still a "blob of tissue" or a "product of conception." They call an unborn baby a "fetus" and fight legislation which attempts to define him/her as a "person." In doing so, they strip away the humanity of the child and place the legal rights of what to do with that "blob" in the hands of the mother alone. This totally takes the father out of the picture. It changes the family structure by removing the man from his headship of the family and placing woman there instead.

The whole issue is couched in terms of "choice" and a woman's right to do what she wants with "her body." Most states have diminished legal constraints concerning parental notification or trimester limitations because a woman's "choice" must be protected more completely. Whether the baby is "viable" is also a fictitious litmus test. The Supreme Court began by using this term to craft a "license to kill" based on whether the baby could survive outside the mother's womb. The Court wanted everyone to believe that no one could know when life began, so "viability" could become the defining factor of life. Using this terminology, the pro-abortion forces launched verbal artillery that objectified the child as a non-living thing that was unable to survive outside the mother's body until it was actually born.

So "viability" became the screen behind which they hid the truth that life begins at conception—and even more visibly, that unborn babies can feel pain and are able to survive at ages much younger than you'd think. Babies deemed "unviable" are aborted past the 20-week mark even though hospitals are routinely saving babies born prematurely at 24, 23, and even 22 weeks. Dozens of mothers have made YouTube videos about such miracle babies, and yet abortionists insist we believe the unborn "fetus" is just tissue with no feelings or life inside. There is no person to protect.

.Not that the Supreme Court should be trusted to define personhood or rights. The first time the Supreme Court came down on the wrong side of an issue of personhood was in the Dred Scott case. Then the Court decided blacks were property and, whether free or slave, could therefore not be citizens of the United States. When slavery ended, for the second time the Court ignored the 14th Amendment and decided, through *Plessy v. Ferguson*, to uphold racial segregation in public facilities.

It is not surprising then, that for the third time in *Roe v. Wade*, the Supreme Court ignored the 14th Amendment by removing the personhood of the baby. The highest court in the land again placed a class of America's citizenry in a category that allowed them to be disposed of, with no regard to any rights the Constitution or our Creator might have already given them. Cloaking babies in the fictional right to "privacy," which the Court said is found in the mother's womb, a whole class of American citizens was stripped of its humanity. This is eerily reminiscent of the way slavery stripped blacks of their humanity and dealt with them according to property law.

Always careful to frame the debate in terms that support women's rights, though, the pro-abortion forces have taken great care to subtly harden the hearts of women toward their children. They have gone to great lengths to erase the hope that most little girls have from childhood – to be a wife and mom. They have framed children as problems, nuisances, and burdens which interfere with a woman's ability to pursue her career or education. No longer is the baby the focus of pregnancy. Instead, all eyes are on the mother who is the decision maker, the judge who determines whether the child is allowed to continue living or be put to death. In place of the husband or father of the child, America is commonly told that abortion is a private decision between "a woman and her doctor," even though most abortionists are not "her doctor." Most never even see the mother until they are between her legs performing the procedure.

An unfortunate repercussion of this culture shift has been the response of the Christian community. There are some among us that identify themselves as Christians who override their consciences and the Scriptures to engage in the culture's acceptance of abortion as a viable option for family planning. Planned Parenthood has engaged pastors all across America to teach and preach abortion's acceptance. One pastor from Atlanta even exclaimed that Planned Parenthood made him a *better* pastor because he is not an "expert on sexuality."[31]

Pastors such as this one rarely preach about the sin of promiscuity and abortion favoring messages that make their parishioners feel good. Scriptures such as Esau and Jacob's struggle in their mother's womb (Genesis 25) or John the Baptist leaping for joy in Mary's womb (Luke 2) are relegated to the great stories of the Bible with little significance related to life today. As society has migrated away from cherishing children, pastors rarely rehearse the tenets of Psalms 127:4-5 which declares children are blessings. Too frequently we hear "I am personally pro-life, but cannot tell a woman what to do with her body." If a pastor dares brave the waters of abortion, most sermons will mirror the culture and the 1 out of 3 post-abortive women sitting in the pews will not be confronted with what the Bible says about life and children.

Convincing the Christian community to stand strong on pro-life is one thing, but even more difficult is convincing people of what most black pro-life leaders believe is the core of the abortion agenda – controlling the birth rate of communities of color in general, and blacks in particular. Abortion is perceived as being a voluntary action on the part of the mother. In most cases, it is believed that women are *choosing to go* into the abortion chamber rather than being driven into it. The line between choice and targeting is frequently blurred, so much so, that few recognize the heinous eugenic foundation upon which abortion stands.

In fact, some blacks have even bought the lie that abortion is *saving* the black community, not just economically because there are fewer mouths to feed, but physically because more women are now being cared for by real doctors. One blogger on RH Reality check said, "*A*ccess to abortion actually saved lives in black communities, where illegal abortion was a leading cause of death before *Roe v. Wade.*"[32] Even pro-abortion statisticians long ago debunked the

---

[31] http://www.plannedparenthoodaction.org/get-involved/vital-service-1143.htm

idea that abortion was a leading cause of death of women before *Roe v. Wade*. But that fact is very much irrelevant to those bent on keeping abortion legal under all circumstances. In fact, there is very little that the pro-abortion community says that is anchored in facts. There is more that is covered up and swept away than is exposed by those in this community.

A close examination of the industry reveals the underbelly of abortion to be a malevolent force still launched by elitists in the furtherance of population control. To disguise their true intent, SisterSong and others use terms that would resonate with communities of color like "reproductive justice" and "reproductive freedom." These are discussion points in civil rights centers such as Atlanta. America hears that "poor and low income" women lack "access" to "reproductive healthcare." Accusations against pro-lifers say they are denying reproductive justice to black women.

Pro-life forces then fail to correct this language, allowing America to accept the idea that abortion is a civil right akin to what blacks fought for during the Jim Crow era, or the fight women mounted to gain property and voting rights. It is ironic that today abortion is seen as being at the core of minority freedom. However there is no evidence that I could find that civil rights leaders of yesterday supported that belief. There is however, evidence that some groups viewed it as a tool that would keep blacks and women in pain and misery.

I actually had a dream about how the abortion forces have framed the debate. I saw their soldiers lined up on one side of the street, firing machine guns at pro-life warriors. Their bullets were their words. With rapid fire, they were firing the words "my body, my choice," and "women's right to choose", and "product of conception," and "fetus." As their words hit us, they penetrated. Along the pro-life lines, our warriors were picking up the spent shells of the abortionists and lobbing them back - with their hands. "It's not a choice, it's a child!" we said. But "choice" was what was cemented in the minds and hearts of the people. Then we picked up the word "fetus" and threw it back at them. But it was "fetus" which was imprinted in our vocabulary, making the baby an object

---

[32]http://www.rhrealitycheck.org/blog/2010/03/03/loretta-ross-unmasks-black-antiabortion-message-media-spin

rather than a person. Time after time, our volleys reinforced the pro-abortion rhetoric rather than penetrating it or tearing it down.

When I woke up, I knew we had to retake the ground that had been surrendered in framing the issue of life. We had to become more adept at framing the argument, calling abortion what it is – the termination of a God- ordained life. We had to stop using their rhetoric as a part of our response, and had to clearly state what they were doing. We had to fight like men. We would take careful aim, then launch the new weapons God had given us, and for which they would be unprepared.

Action Steps

1. **Identify** the rhetoric of the abortionist – i.e. lack of access, fetus, my body, my choice, reproductive justice, etc.

2. **Practice** phrases which are opposite of their rhetoric, but clearly defines the issue.

3. **Look** for opportunities to insert the words of life into the discussions of abortion wherever possible.

4. **Pray** for God to end the scourge of abortion in this nation.

Chapter 6: Outreach

The average person knows that in the black community, the church is a hub of influence. Many will regale you with tales about pastors who worked with Martin Luther King, Jr. to launch the Civil Rights movement in America. Others will tell you all about the political steps their pastors have taken to influence the culture on behalf of their sheep. So it was a no-brainer to begin the pro-life education process by reaching out to pastors across the nation, beginning with those I knew in Georgia.

Reaching the black community has proven difficult for many mainstream pro-life organizations. The civil and women's rights movements have been used to create an environment of distrust, categorizing pro-life abolitionists as an arm of Republican politics and obfuscating the moral issue in political rhetoric. Moreover, pro-abortion forces have been very aggressive in recruiting black leaders to speak in opposition to the pro-life movement – hiring the likes of Carlton Veazy and Vanessa Cullen, black spokespeople who are paid hundreds of thousands of dollars to promote abortion and contraception while railing against pro-life activists. They have taken great care to recruit friends in the media to portray pro-life abolitionists as extremists and pro-abortion advocates as mainstream.

Pro-life organizations, for their part, have not committed the same level of resources to reaching the black community. In fact, while some have hired blacks in attempts to do outreach, many have not fully funded their initiatives or committed an appropriate number of years to complete the outreach. So most efforts fail to penetrate the targeted audience, and many of the black advocates who work with the established pro-life organizations have been handicapped right out of the gate.

Yet, while working with these national leaders, Georgia Right to Life (GRTL) approached me about coming to work with them come January 1, 2009. Specifically, they wanted to do an outreach to the black community, and I agreed it was a need I could help meet. In the coming days and months, I would come to appreciate the work the Lord was sending me to do. My journey to make the sanctity of life a politically urgent issue for the black community had begun. That sounds quite lovely – make the sanctity of life a politically urgent issue for the black community. But it has not been easy, no matter how lovely it sounds.

When I began my outreach with Georgia Right To Life, I was naïve enough to believe that all I had to do was make the call and I could at least get to speak with the black pastors we intended to reach. Not so. I called and called but got no response. I learned the hard way that in order to reach a pastor, you have to know someone that can introduce you. Most pastors are pursued every day by a host of salesmen, folk that believe they have the answers to whatever question the pastor might think of, and those who are in want of financial or other support. So as a means of survival, they don't meet with everyone who comes along. However, if you are introduced to the pastor by someone the pastor trusts, you can have his or her ear.

So I did what I always do when I am stumped by something: I prayed. As I prayed about what to do, I got a revelation. Women are not usually so hard to reach, so I called my female ministry friends for help and, lo and behold, the doors slowly began to open.

I hosted breakfasts and teas, luncheons, and dinners for pastor's wives and female ministers. I called on Congressmen with whom I had relationship to host breakfasts for me, and I invited as many leaders as I could to come and learn about the impact of abortion on the black community. Although it was slow going, each week the turnouts increased. All around the state of Georgia, more and more blacks were learning about abortion's adverse impact.

Not one of the pastors that I met turned me away in disbelief. In fact, it was just the opposite. Pastors were alarmed by the information; most expressing they had no idea that abortion was an issue for the black community. One pastor felt so strongly about the information I shared, he actually allowed me to speak to his congregation on Mother's Day. More and more churches began to open their doors and over the course of my first year, I visited churches in Augusta, Stockbridge, Savannah, Athens, Gainesville, Douglas, and Stone Mountain, to name a few.

Reaching out to the historically black colleges and universities (HBCU) in metropolitan Atlanta was another goal I set, and soon I was able to do my first presentation at Morehouse College. I did not know that an HBCU like Morehouse had a college Republican group that was excited about my message. I had met a couple of their representatives at a luncheon, and I was overjoyed when they extended an invitation for me to speak. But the meeting at Morehouse turned into an adventure like right out of a novel!

As I walked to the building where the meeting was to be held, a section of recently drilled sidewalk grabbed my heel and threw me to the ground!! My cell phone, which I happened to be carrying, flew to the left of me, my papers to the right. So there I was, this supposedly dignified black woman, sprawled on the ground, thinking how grateful I was that I was wearing pants. Even though my neck hurt, my left wrist was sprained, and I was generally bruised and battered, I carried on. Once I successfully navigated the rest of the distance to the building, I was able to present and persuade at least a few of those present to rethink their position on terminating the lives of children in the womb.

That first invitation lead to more invitations. For more than a year, I was frequently invited back to Morehouse to discuss abortion in various venues. At one event, the college Republicans arranged for a panel discussion that included a philosophy professor. I was shocked, literally, by some of his comments such as a person can lose his/her personhood when he/she becomes incapacitated. He was advocating for terminating the lives of those who could not care for themselves—those he deemed incapable of living a quality of life that he alone defined. It was surreal.

It was this forum where I was first introduced to the notion of the child as a "parasite." A young man in the audience began to refer to women as "hosts" whose bodies are intruded upon by babies. No matter how we challenged him, his idea of life in the womb was that the child was akin to an insect that was interfering with someone else's "right to life."

Next the Morehouse Republicans and Spelman Democrats hosted a panel discussion about abortion. How my heart broke when a young woman from Spelman began to shake her hands and push away as she described a friend's desire to abort her child. "Just get it out of me," she said a couple of times. "Just get it out of me." That imagery is stuck in my mind. Some of our young women have been so indoctrinated that they believe the child is an "it" to be gotten rid of, rather than their own personal offspring to be cherished.

As I was leaving the venue, one of the Morehouse gentleman escorted me to my car. As we walked, he told me something that made my tears flow freely. He said Spelman uses money it collects from student fees each year to pay for at least two, and some say four, student abortions. And right outside the gates of Spelman is the billboard which tells those pregnant students the location of the closest place to get that abortion.

The work to educate suddenly seemed to swell before my eyes, becoming a huge almost insurmountable thing, seeking to swallow me up. Realizing that this generation of youth has no idea what it means to live in a culture where it is not acceptable to kill a child in the womb was unnerving. Many of the questions they asked demonstrated that they could not imagine such a thing. They wanted to know if women would be put in jail if abortion was delegalized, or just how it would work. When I suggested that the issue would go back to the states to decide, as it was prior to *Roe vs. Wade*, they looked at me with blank stares, unable to imagine a state that would not allow abortion.

While some of the Morehouse attendees spoke of the baby as an object rather than person, others in the room acknowledged the personhood of the baby in a very impersonal way. It was chilling to hear some of the women talk about aborting a baby with no more compassion or thought than one would give, say, a roach. There was no horror at the idea that abortion takes a life. This is the generation that kills people for sport in arcade games, and it is easy for them to couch their arguments around their desires. They have been so desensitized to the value of life that they can recognize the child in the womb is a life but still take deliberate steps to kill that child. It was and is clear to me that much work is needed if we are to restore sanctity of life in the American culture.

My outreach efforts were broadening by this time. More churches were willing to allow me to come. I even found ministerial alliances that would allow me to speak to several pastors at once. It was at one of these meetings that I had an encounter that, to this day, keeps me motivated to press on. One of the pastors I met from Jonesboro, GA stopped me as we were preparing to leave the meeting and said two things to me: conservatives had a Republican President, a Republican Senate and House. Why then did they not end abortion when they were in control? (While I am still formulating an answer to this, I don't believe most Republicans would want to hear it).

The second thing he said was that when I spoke to pastors, I was to speak with the authority God had given me. I was not *asking* them to help *me*, but giving a directive from God that they had to help end this scourge on our nation. Wow. Those unforgettable words shook me to my roots. I immediately put this advice into practice so that whenever I speak to pastors, I encourage them to fight as a mandate from God.

Thirty-nine years is a long time to fight against the unabated atrocities of the abortion industry. While educating and activating the black community about abortion's impact is a journey, we can't withstand another thirty-nine years of devastation. Depopulation of the black American community has already begun, which we will discuss later. Those involved in the fight so far have not been able to penetrate the barrier of mistrust by the black community of the predominantly white messengers. In fact, many blacks have viewed abortion as a "white" issue that is neither important nor relevant to black culture and progress.

At the urging of the abortion community, blacks remain suspicious even of the blacks who are engaged in the fight. The pro-abortion activists paint us as puppets of the white man who pulls our strings to create a racial impact where none exists. Many of these activists proclaim that we are sellouts, "Uncle Toms," and the like.

Overcoming this dogma is part of the fight for those engaged in pro-life activities. Doing outreach under these misrepresentations and lies is yet another front on which anti-abortionists must fight. But it is worth it when women are freed from the lies. It is worth it when one more foot soldier engages in the war against the depopulation of communities of color.

Action Steps

1. **Approach** your Pastor and engage in a discussion of abortion's impact on communities of color.

2. **Invite** pro-life leaders to address the issue at your church, men and/or women's conference, or other outreach event.

3. **Volunteer** with a pro-life organization such as CareNet or Heartbeat International to reach abortion-minded women.

4. **Pray** that abortion will be ended in America and around the world.

Chapter 7. Deploying the Troops

I logged thousands of miles as I traveled the state and the nation, telling everyone who would listen about the devastation of abortion. I promised people I would come again, even if there were only two who wanted to hear the message, and I really meant it—then and now. The fact is, abortion has so infiltrated almost every crevice of black life that its devastation can be seen at almost every turn. Many hearts have been hardened and desensitized. Every day, the death toll reaches into the thousands as society demonstrates its lack of regard for the sanctity of life.

One glaring example of this can be found in Chicago's murder rate over the 2012 Memorial Day weekend. There were 40 shootings that resulted in 10 homicides. This is a common occurrence there: in April 2010, 40 were shot and 4 killed; in June that same year, 52 were shot and 7 killed.[33] That means more people were killed on the streets of Chicago than died in the active war zone of Afghanistan or Iraq that same weekend! A few weeks after that, ten young people between the ages of 10-18 were shot during a weekend event in Indiana. It has become clear that this generation is so used to death, they can play video games that score points for killing the old and infirm while the real shootings on their urban streets barely register in their minds. It seems likely that an unintended consequence of abortion has been the diminishing sanctity of life overall.

I continued to zigzag the state and nation in my efforts to educate. Trying to increase my connections in the community, I frequently attended events hosted by special interest groups and others. One such event was the Tavis Smiley Atlanta Accountability Tour. At the beginning of the event, we learned that earlier that week, Smiley's Executive Producer, Cheryl Flowers, lost her fight with a most extreme form of breast cancer. Tavis took a moment to eulogize her and as he recounted the impact she'd had

---

[33]   http://www.huffingtonpost.com/2010/06/21/chicago-violence-at-least_n_619259.html

on his life, I leaned toward a new friend and wondered aloud if Tavis knew of the link between breast cancer and abortion. My friend literally paled, if black men can pale. Then he asked me to explain what I meant.

I offered him the Cliff's Notes explanation: that in 27 of 40 studies, there is a documented 50% breast cancer risk increase by age 45 for women who have had an induced abortion. He did not know that among women with a family history of breast cancer (mother, grandmother, sister, or aunt), the increase in risk was 80%. If the woman had her abortion before she was 18, the increase in risk was more than 100% (doubled)![34]

At the conclusion of my whispered explanation, my new friend explained that he had lost a child through abortion and that the mom had died from breast cancer at an early age, younger than 45. I am ashamed and saddened to say that while I mumbled "I'm sorry," I quickly changed the subject from this personal confession toward a more general conversation. I am frequently pained by this memory, having lost the opportunity to grieve his loss with him in order to change the subject and make myself more comfortable. I now wonder *what if* I had not done that but had stopped to mourn his loss with him? *What if*, instead of pushing those emotions back, I had allowed the tears which were threatening, to actually flow? *What if* I had allowed him to work through whatever emotions he was feeling in my presence, rather than diverting the conversation and leaving him to mourn at some later time when I would not see his pain? *What if . . . ?* It's a very real but hard question to which I cannot find a suitable answer. That moment is gone and cannot be claimed again.

The very next day, I went to Selma, Alabama with Dr. Alveda King, niece of Dr. Martin Luther King, Jr. and daughter of Rev. A. D. King to walk across the historic Edmund Pettus Bridge. This time we walked for the sake of the unborn. As I made the first step onto the bridge, I literally felt the presence of those who had come before me. I could almost see that historic day in March of 1965 as I was overcome with the presence of those who had marched for equal rights over forty years ago. I heard them in my heart, urging me to not give up the fight for life. I could almost hear them saying

[34] http://www.aaplog.org/complications-of-induced-abortion/induced-abortion-and-breast-cancer/

"March on, fight on! Your work is not in vain!" I tangibly felt a mantle fall to my shoulders as we slowly walked, and it was not until I was midway across the bridge that I was able to gather myself. I never had an experience like that before—a calling. That feeling which gripped me on the bridge is with me even now.

It was because of these two events that I began to measure what if any effect we could have if we began to frame the pro-life argument from the perspective of the baby—from his/her paramount right to life. I wondered *what if* we employed the arsenal of nonviolent weapons, left to us by those who fathered America's Civil Rights Movement? *What if* we accepted the mantle to fight on, left to us by those who had marched before us on the Pettus Bridge? *What if* we declared a moratorium on abortion and held sit-ins at one or more of the clinics on a Saturday, the abortionists' busiest day—or a Thursday, which is the busiest day for late term abortions?

What if we were to boycott those big businesses that fund Planned Parenthood, the organization which targets blacks for extermination in their abortion mills? *What if* we organized today's version of freedom riders to ride from Maine to California, for the lives of the unborn and women harmed by abortion? In my heart, I added the following tactics to the arsenal I was building: 1) uniting with other black pro-life leaders in support of a unified message of life; 2) forming coalitions with other like-minded groups, without regard to their partisanship; 3) examining history to see what worked in the fight for civil rights and what did not. Yes, I felt like I was onto something in my street fight for life.

On the Georgia Right To Life home front, regional meetings were planned and executed in preparation for the legislative initiative that would be introduced in January 2010. Strategies were developed which would ensure grassroots participation when needed. It was at one of these regional meetings, that Ryan Bomberger showed up, and the game was on.

Let me take a moment to tell you how I met Ryan Bomberger. I believe it was a divine appointment, one that destined us to be an intricate part of changing America's culture back toward sanctity of life. Five or six months prior, while I was navigating the obstacles of getting into black churches, I accepted the requests of videographers wanting to film me, telling my story. One videographer, Chad Bonham, producer of *Life Happens*, after recording a segment with me, asked me if I knew a young man named Ryan Bomberger. I had not met him, and I said so. Chad told me how Ryan's birth mother had been raped but chose to carry him to term and place him for adoption. Ryan had then been adopted by a Mennonite family in Pennsylvania and had 14 siblings! Wow. Chad encouraged me to reach out to Ryan. After some more prompting, I did.

Ryan and I had an instant connection, and our passion for pro-life dominated our lunch conversation as we shared about our work. We found we had common thoughts about abortion, and both of us believed that if the government were to place people on an endangered species list, black babies would certainly top the list. We thought this was especially true in Georgia, where black women had been getting more than 50% percent of total abortions for years.

Once I learned of Ryan's trailblazing expertise in branding and graphic design, I hoped he could somehow help reframe the debate so that abortion as a norm would be uprooted. I had given a lot of thought to the best ways of penetrating the Church, and had written action plans that could be implemented as my work progressed. I sent two of the plans to Ryan after that lunch – the first one was a presentation that aimed to reclaim the legacy of the black community. It encouraged them to remember the genius intrinsic in blacks. The second one was coined "Operation Outrage." It was a campaign to expose the outrageousness of the abortion industry. I hoped that sharing these plans with Ryan would help stimulate his creative genius. I was convinced that his graphic communication skills could fully convey the truth about abortion's detrimental impact.

Fast forward several months to our meeting at Georgia Right to Life, as we casually discussed how things were going, Ryan quietly pulled up a graphic on his computer. Turning it so I could see, I saw a graphic that in one glance displayed both Ryan's and my heart about the impact of abortion on the black community: looking at me was this beautiful black child. Some say he looks like he is about to cry. Others say he looks worried. All agree he definitely looked as if he is contemplating serious issues. Above his head in a vibrant yellow is the caption, "Black Children are an Endangered Species." Below his face is the lamentation, "TooManyAborted.com". Wow. Wow. Wow. It exactly expressed what was in my heart. With a sense of urgency, I beckoned to Dan Becker, President of GRTL, and asked him to take a look. The image was provocative. It was out of the box. It was a message worth conveying on a billboard. Thus began the auspicious billboard campaign that was a punch felt round the world!

By late fall, Georgia Right to Life had garnered enough legislator support for us to proceed with our bill. We hired an attorney to craft a bill to protect babies based on race and gender. This attorney was a former legislator who was familiar with the internal workings of Georgia's legislative process. This crafting of a civil rights bill for a baby in utero was a tall order that required a great deal of thought and input. We referred to the bill drafted by Congressman Trent Franks called the Prenatal Nondiscrimination Act (PRNDA). It served as the skeleton upon which we built our legislation. We had to tweak the original wording to capture the vision they had of a bill protecting unborn babies in a manner similar to the way black people's rights were protected by the Civil Rights Act.

Unfortunately, the bill provided by the former legislator fell short of the high hopes we all had. And we were back to square one, looking to craft a new bill to fit the equal protection parameters of the Constitution while affording some measure of protection to children in the womb. It was not until January that we were finally able to pull the bill together.

GRTL recruited a legislator to craft the bill, who I fully believe is Georgia's 21st century Wilbur Wilberforce for life. Within a 48-hour period, Ed Setzler and his legislative counsel wrote a bill that is probably the most vetted piece of pro-life legislation in the country. When I read the bill, I literally began to cry… and then whoop and holler because it was/is what I had envisioned. We suddenly had a bill of the same magnitude, in my opinion, as the Civil Rights Bill of 1964. It was a law that would not only protect unborn babies, but provide a measure of protection to the mother as well. Our carefully devised legislation was circulated among attorneys across the nation to get input on what would work best at the state level.

The bill was simple—just three pages long when first drafted. It basically forbade the performance of an abortion if the doctor knew the woman was coerced, or sought because of the race/gender of the child. The bill also afforded a woman some relief if the doctor failed to meet the other laws of the state such as the 24-hour waiting period and requisite ultrasound. The thing I loved the most about the bill was that it would provide an opportunity to examine whether the location of the abortion clinics was intentional in order to control the birth rates of blacks, Latinos, and the poor.

Now that we had a bill and the billboard graphics, it was time to outline our next steps. This was where the fun began. We made phone calls to billboard companies, and scheduled meetings with sales representatives. The question on all our minds was if any billboard company would put our billboards up. Our chosen billboard company, after running our ad "up the chain," came back with a reasonable price and a yes. A combination of eighty billboards and posters would be up the second week in January 2010 in Fulton and DeKalb counties, where more than 70% of Georgia's abortions are performed. Next, GRTL and Ryan Bomberger formed a partnership to bring the issue of black abortion the forefront. We were ready to battle.

Needless to say, when the launch week arrived, I eagerly went from site to site to finally see the billboards up in the air. But you have to understand that I am probably the most directionally challenged individual in America. Having no sense of direction, I tell people all the time how grateful I am that God allowed me to be born in the 20th century rather than during slavery. Had I been born during slavery, I would have been leading the people "noph," and God knows we would have been in Mississippi somewhere before I realized I was going in the wrong direction. So not wanting to leave my search to chance, I pulled out my trusty GPS and entered the addresses of the planned billboards.

To my shock and dismay, I could not find one billboard. Anywhere. After putting more than 30 miles on the car looking for them, I finally pulled over and called the office. We were all perplexed since no one had received a call indicating there was a problem. One phone call later however, we found out that the sales rep apparently missed a rung on the ladder, because their corporate office had pulled the approval to put up the boards. Not only did they pull the campaign, but they offered their suggestion as to what our message should say.

We began to research new billboard companies immediately. After all, we had planned to announce the billboard campaign at the annual Memorial Walk for Life at the Georgia Capitol, which was just days away. We had even printed posters of the billboard that could be carried by participants in the crowd. We had also planned an abortion demonstration depicting the thirty-seven years of abortion. In it, a person born in each year since the *Roe* decision would hold a sign indicating the numbers of abortions in that year.

Despite our best efforts to make sure that all our "i's" were dotted and "t's" were crossed, we had hit a brick wall. No-one returned the back-to-back calls we made to rectify the situation, and this caused our frustrations to mount. It was particularly hard to bear after our attorney confirmed that billboard company owners are allowed to decline billboards without violating free speech rights.

We believed our only recourse was to call for a boycott of the businesses which placed advertisements on this company's billboards. We threatened to do exactly that. We also prepared to announce to the 5000-plus marchers gathering, that this company had declined to fulfill their contract with us. And while we were in the Georgia Capitol preparing for our march, there was also an Annual March for Life going on simultaneously in Washington DC. Because we had feet on the ground there too, we were planning to have the same announcement made to the 200,000 people gathering there. We set a deadline of 5:30 that evening to have heard from the billboard company, or else we would go forward with the announcements to boycott.

I waited on pins and needles. My spirit was burdened when the phone did not ring by the deadline. We finalized the message for our folk on the ground in D.C., and just as I was putting the last period on the announcement, the phone rang. It was good news! One of the billboard company's executives visited the website TooManyAborted.com and found it credible. The billboards were set to go up the following Monday. At the 2010 Memorial Walk for Life, we were able to announce our success in launching the first-ever-of-its-kind billboard campaign. When the crowd watched the 37 years of abortion played out before them, tears came to many eyes. From the 37-year old to the infant in the womb, Georgia was visually displaying abortion's impact on an entire generation of people. Now it was time to take the fight to the next level in the corridors of power – the State Capitol.

With the billboards in place, we knew we had an edge this time. After firing up my trusty GPS, I found each billboard I searched for, and I knew the fight was on. Anticipating a tumultuous reaction to the billboards, we waited with baited breath for the calls and emails. But nothing happened. The billboards were up for over a week and there was not one peep from the communities involved or the media. We did not even get a phone call asking about the boards. Amazing!

So we organized a press conference inviting members of Georgia's print, television, and radio media to join us at the Capitol where we would announce the billboards. We also invited prominent black pro-life leaders to join us in making the announcement. We set up the conference site, prepared our press packets, and made everything ready for those who might come. And to our dismay, no media outlet accepted the invitation—not *one* journalist came. We did not let that deter us. We conducted the conference as if they had all shown up, and we pressed forward with our announcement of the billboards and legislation.

What we had not anticipated was that one of the journalists would blog a story about the campaign even though he was unable to attend. He included a graphic of the billboard and accused us of targeting black women. Despite this erroneous assertion, we knew we had made the right choice in the billboard campaign because the graphic he printed provoked a reaction that erupted into a firestorm which swept the city of Atlanta, the state, the nation, and the world.

Within 24 hours of the blog article, I received a call to come on MSNBC. Scheduled with me was a representative from SisterSong, the Women of Color Reproductive Justice Collective. Just a few weeks before, I had reached out to this organization and requested a meeting to discuss our differences on whether there has been a genocidal impact of abortion on the black community.

But at that time, I did not realize they were the primary proponent of abortion in the African-American community in Atlanta.

I was shocked to not only hear the representative's praise of abortion, but to hear her say that abortion was a positive tool that rescued blacks from poverty! From this first meeting at MSNBC until our last encounter in legislative session, this was the song SisterSong sang – that abortion rights lifts us from the depths of our socioeconomic circumstances. Who knew?

The next interview after MSNBC came within hours of the first. This time it was the *New York Times*. This interview helped me to learn and understand the language of the media as it relates to the pro-life and pro-abortion struggle. They always refer to pro-life advocates as anti-abortion because there is a negative connotation to positions labeled "anti-x." Alternatively, they always refer to the anti-life advocate as pro-choice. In this sense they are trained to promote one agenda over the other. They cast the pro-life community as extreme and the pro-abortion community as the norm.

The reporter took care to cast doubt on our assertions of abortions' disproportionate impact in how she wrote the article. Using the same rhetoric of the abortion industry, she suggested federal data did not support our stance and stated there was little evidence of our claims. This time I figured out how to couch my language to combat the media's bias against me.

When the billboard story caught hold, which was immediately after that first blog, media outlet after media outlet picked up the story and more and more of the extreme advocates for abortion revealed their minds and hearts regarding the sanctity of life. The weapon most frequently deployed by those for abortion was the weapon of deflection. Their habit was to change the conversation to a discussion of women's rights, reproductive health, women's health, or social justice concerns—away from the baby's right to life. They encourage their army to never allow the conversation to rest on the numbers of abortions in the black community.

One of the most frequent charges leveled against our billboards was that we personally were attacking, shaming black women. They were careful to make arguments that we did not trust black women to make their own decisions about their reproductive health. Their goal is always to keep the eyes of the nation toward accepting unfettered abortion on demand. Since the first billboard, they have organized a new partnership under SisterSong called Trust Black Women. They exist, they say, "to ensure that Black women have the human right to make our own decisions about our reproductive lives, and that we should never regret difficult choices based on our complicated experiences."[35]

But one of the things these feminists fear most is that black women would *understand* the numerical impact abortion is having on the culture. So they make claims that black women such as Day Gardner, Alveda King, and I are trying to act as the slave masters did, disguising our true racist intent in a false sense of compassion. Their agenda of abortion at all costs cannot withstand the scrutiny that will come once blacks understand the underlying agenda of abortion in America. So they labeled us "anti-women" and took care to always respond by changing the conversation into a discussion of women's rights.

Planned Parenthood had a different response to the wave of media calling attention to the abortion numbers. This time they said black women experience more unplanned pregnancies than other ethnicities, and as a result, have more abortions. I first heard this in Washington when we demanded the defunding of Planned Parenthood in 2009. For the sake of the discussion, let's assume this statement to be true. It still does not explain why black women are "choosing" to terminate the lives of their children more than other ethnicities. It does not explain what is drawing the black woman into the abortion den rather than toward keeping her child.

This, of course, is what needs exposing. Abortionists want to disassociate from the founder of Planned Parenthood's eugenic background and the whole context of racism that "family planning" was constructed around. They paint Margaret Sanger as a product of her time and ignore the many instances in which she characterized particular ethnicities, especially blacks, as "weeds and misfits." They also ignore her successor who was a leading eugenicist, and the racial implications of trying to extinguish poverty and overpopulation through abortion on demand. In

[35]http://sistersong.net/index.php?option=com_content&view=article&id=41&Itemid=78

other words, they ignore the history—the facts which are staring them in the face.

Action Steps

1. **Familiarize** yourself with the language of the anti-life community such as SisterSong

2. **Find** and or prepare talking points that spotlight the deceit of their message

3. **Find** resources in your community, including capable speakers to share the pro-life message

4. **Help** pro-life organizations put up billboards and other media with the life message

5. **Pray** that God will end the scourge of abortion in America

Chapter 8: New Weapons

When Georgia Right to Life began to formulate its 2010 legislative agenda, I wondered aloud if one of the new weapons available to us would be to craft a piece of legislation that would protect the baby based on its race or gender. In fact my conversations with Ryan Bomberger and others about black children being "endangered" came from the thoughts I was mulling over about the Endangered Species Act—a bill that went to great lengths to protect animals.

I found it ironic that America would clamor to lock up, say, Michael Vick for dog fighting, but would not lock up the abortionist for the violence committed against children in the womb. A few thousand animal rights activists in America hold demonstrations where they chant and scream for the end of cruelty to baby animals. However, I don't ever recall seeing one of them come out to protest abortion's cruelty to baby humans. If America can go to such extremes to protect animals, certainly it can take affirmative steps to protect children in the womb.

I actually looked at the language of the Endangered Species Act along with the Civil Rights Act to see if any of its language could be adapted. I called Alveda King and explored her memories of how her uncle and father developed their ideas for the Civil Rights Act of 1964. I wanted to find out how they did it. Did the lawyers write it and come present it to the Kings? Or did the Kings write it and then present it to the lawyers to make it fit, within legal parameters?

With these kinds of questions swirling in my mind, I eagerly attended the Georgia Right to Life legislative meetings to discuss what bill would be offered. Emails flew back and forth for a number of days, which then turned into weeks and even months as we explored options. There were factors that had to be considered, the most glaring of which centered on the question of raising race in the piece of legislation. Any time a white Republican raises race in any conversation, alarms go off. Most are afraid to even say anything about a racial matter for fear of being labeled. And the reality is that some Republicans *and* Democrats still have racial bias and prejudice. Addressing an issue from a racial perspective understandably causes a face to face battle with their prejudices.

Georgia was one of the leading segregated states in the Jim Crow south. What came out of Georgia reverberated across the south and many times across the nation. We knew we could not be naïve about race still being a factor in the political process. For example, some might not have wanted to restrict abortions based on race because they would want to take their daughter to the abortionist if she was raped or had been impregnated by a black man, whether consensual or not.

Our questions had to be answered as we navigated the waters of developing and passing legislation that would provide protection to unborn babies, especially based on race and gender. We had to stretch ourselves to anticipate every side of the matter. We really wanted people to understand the disproportionate impact of abortion by race in our state especially.

At the same time we were holding these discussions, we also had to garner the support of the pro-life legislators for other bills that GRTL introduced. A closed door meeting was held in St. Simons Island, GA. At that meeting, seasoned national pro-life attorneys met with the pro-life Republicans to discuss the ramifications of a bill that would challenge *Roe v. Wade.* Commitments were made and promises given that this was the year to take a principled stand for life, even if it challenged a legislator's future political career. Surprisingly, Georgia Right to Life came away with what they believed to be a solid commitment. Legislators on our side said they would make the 2010 pro-life legislation their last stand if need be.

Senate Bill 529 was crafted during these discussions with legislators and others from around the country. The idea of a civil rights bill for the unborn was no longer a theory related to endangered species or even the Civil Rights Act. This bill not only challenged the status quo surrounding abortion, but provided a path of recourse for women and babies harmed at the abortionist's hand. Not only was race covered, but so were coercion, gender and targeting. It was the ideal bill that addressed the injustices heaped on women under the guise of ensuring women's rights.

In addition to legislation that might challenge the racial impact of abortion, we looked for other resources that would help make the case that there was a deliberate targeting of the black community by the abortion industry. One new weapon had already come to light in June of 2009. Life Dynamics, a pro-life organization in Denton, Texas, had introduced a documentary called *Maafa 21*. The *Maafa*, which means "great tragedy" in Swahili, pointed out the death rate of blacks by abortion since *Roe v. Wade*. The movie took the viewer on a journey of discovery beginning with Charles Darwin, Francis Galton, and others, and then ended with Planned Parenthood's continuing efforts to increase abortion in black areas. As I met the leaders of various ministerial alliances across the state, *Maafa 21* quickly became a leading resource I could leave in their hands, especially when they agreed to host screenings in their churches and community centers.

We were looking for other new weapons. In 2010, I had joined forces with Priests for Life, a major organization that had been fighting for the lives of children across the nation by launching pro-life freedom rides in Birmingham, Alabama. Black and white pro-life leaders from across the country joined Father Frank Pavone and Alveda King at a rally on the eve of the first Pro-Life Freedom Ride. *At the rally, time was given to* memorialize all the lives which were ended by abortion, including those of the mothers who had died at the abortionists' hands. And every care was taken to make room for the healing of various wounds inflicted by America's greatest tragedy, second only to slavery. The rally was held on a Friday in front of the Birmingham Jefferson Convention Center, followed by a prayer vigil in front of the Birmingham Planned Parenthood. High on the success of the rally, on Saturday morning we rolled onto Auburn Avenue in Atlanta, Georgia.

As we pulled up to the Martin Luther King, Jr. burial chamber, planning to place a wreath there and pray, we were dashed with the cold water of today's political bias. **We were denied the opportunity to place the wreath and were in fact told that if we set it down we would be arrested.** We were told that, earlier in the day, barricades had been placed to stop us from even walking in front of the wading pool! We were allowed to be ushered quickly by the crypt, but we could not stop, we could not pray, we could not even stand and reflect. Park guards stationed along the way were screaming instructions to keep moving, and reminding us with almost every step that the wreath was not to be set down lest we face arrest.

Believing we had the freedom (the absence of necessity, coercion, or constraint in choice or action) to pray on the grounds of the "new" Ebenezer Church, we walked across the street. Again our path was blocked and we were accosted by the park staff to the point of the megaphone being snatched, unceremoniously, from the hand of Father Pavone who was beginning to lead prayer. As we regrouped to determine what we should do, my passion and anger began to rise.

I realized the rights of free speech and assembly that enabled civil rights protesters on the streets of Birmingham and Selma, Alabama to convene and protest America's segregation laws were now being violated by a contingent of the federal government that had once provided protection to those who were protesting. And they did this at the gravesite of the man who had led the fight. Federal agents who had once been dispatched to ensure freedom of speech and peaceful assembly in America were now denying that same right. We could not peacefully assemble and place a wreath, pray, or reflect anywhere on the grounds of the *federally* funded Martin Luther King National Historic Site. Finally, we were forced across the street on what we were told was "public" property where we prayed and sang.

But this was not because it was new policy, or because there were some terrorist threat. It was simply because we were on the wrong side of the political propaganda. Those who had gathered to "protest" us were permitted to boisterously assemble. They were provided a shaded area, replete with seating, on the grounds of the "new" Ebenezer. They were allowed to heckle, to chant, to hurl abusive phrases at us through their bullhorn which was not confiscated from them, as they stood on federal property. The federal government which had once protected the rights of those that marched, those that memorialized the lives that had been lost in lynching and others killings, was now the wielder of influence that blocked peaceful demonstrations against a moral wrong—the taking of innocent lives.

Now some of you may feel that what happened to us at the Martin Luther King National Park should not be placed in the same category as the violence that was perpetrated through the days of Jim Crow, especially since those protesting our pro-life presence were black. But I disagree. The violence perpetrated in the abortion mills across the country is much worse than that of Jim Crow. You see, *millions* did not die on those southern streets. Our families fought to ensure we remained alive, healthy, and able to live full lives once we were really free of racial constraints. That same hand of racism which lynched blacks and tortured Emmet Till for supposedly flirting with a white woman, is the same hand now reaching into the wombs of women and ripping the lives of their children into tiny pieces, to be discarded like common waste.

So while the National Park Service was busy violating our first amendment right to peacefully assemble, the protestors were loudly chanting their dissent through their megaphone. Ignoring the fact that a significant number of those on the Freedom Ride were black, the protesters acted as if those present were all white and they were angry and offended that we sang "We Shall Overcome." Despite the presence of Naomi and Alveda King, they were angry and offended that we sought to show our respects at the tomb of Martin Luther King. The blacks protesters were defiant in their anger, believing we had no "right to co-opt" the civil rights legacy.

Co-opt the civil rights legacy - what does that mean?! This shift in attitude of some blacks is not just surprising, but stunning! Since when did terminating the lives of babies become a civil right? The civil rights movement that I remember brought national attention to the horrific impact of slavery and Jim Crow. Martyrs like Emmet Till put a face on the inhumane treatment of blacks in the south and around the nation. It demanded an end to government sanctioned, institutionalized racism. But abortion has taken the place of Jim Crow, and is now cloaked in a garment of acceptability that includes government sanctioned, institutionalized discrimination.

We later learned that permits had been applied for but denied to us, the Pro-life Freedom Riders who are black and white. The money paid to secure the permit was verbally approved but ultimately returned. Yet anti-life protesters were permitted and given complete approval to voice their dissent against us, days after the permit holders had turned our requests down.

We were there to honor the man we believe understood that while God is our source, our children are our strength, lineage, and potential for political and social power. We wanted to recognize the strength he passed on to us at the cost of his life, by laying a wreath at his tomb. However, those at the park were too vested in being Democrat than American or black. They were more interested in defending the pro-abortion agenda than protecting the rights of those whose voices have been silenced by the atrocity of abortion.

They were actually co-opting civil rights, not us. The civil rights era I remember draped itself in the principles expounded in the Bible. It did not subordinate itself to the political dogma of ungodly principles such as those found in today's Democrat Party. Never were we defined by whether or not we supported ungodly principles over all others – until now. Many blacks are so busy being Democrat we have forgotten our roots and what it means to be black. We no longer protect one another and our interests. We have succumbed to a dogma that has true racists shouting with glee because we participate in our own destruction.

I am sure that had the Freedom Ride buses arrived earlier, we would have seen the white women of Planned Parenthood doling out signs and other protest paraphernalia to their black "sisters." We would have seen who really is behind these protests to keep killing black babies in the womb. We could have observed for ourselves how the puppet masters pulled the strings of those unfortunate women—black women who were dancing the macabre dance of a woman's right to choose.

Partnering with the National Black Pro-life Coalition, we launched another new weapon—the first of its kind—a Day of Mourning, across eighteen states. Black leaders hosted press conferences to urge state and federal legislators to defund Planned Parenthood and investigate the deliberate targeting of blacks and other communities of color. Each participating state was encouraged to have at least twenty-five blacks openly stand against abortion, Planned Parenthood, and its population control agenda.

Another precedent-setting weapon was the Sampson Project. Besides the church, there are other spheres of influence that can be tapped in order to reach significant numbers of blacks. One leading venue of influence is the barber shop and hair salon. The moral and political discussions held there are legendary, stuff movies are made of (as in *Barber Shop I & II*, and *Beauty Shop*). The Sampson Project was an outreach to barbers and hair stylists in the hopes that if we could inject the truth about pro-life into barber shop talk, we could start to uproot the pro-abortion mentality.

So we went to the Disney World of the black hair industry, the Bronner Brothers Hair Show in Atlanta. This company, founded in 1947, conducts a spectacular trade show annually. It attracts more than 50,000 barbers and stylists from around the world each year. They come for the continuing education classes, cutting edge products, camaraderie, and pure hair pageantry. So we staffed our booth at the show with seasoned, pro-life advocates who could convey our message effectively. We encouraged the barbers and stylists to set aside abortion rhetoric in order to have an open discussion about abortion's impact on the black community. As a result of our outreach, more than 1,000 stylists from 34 states agreed to watch *Maafa21*, and most importantly, discuss it with their patrons. Some even said they would show the documentary right in their shops.

Then we rented a billboard not far from the show so that the 50,000 attendees would see the billboard message: "Betrayed! AbortionInTheHood.com." Within days of going up, hotels in the area began calling to have the board removed.

Our message was being heard, and it was disturbing. We knew we were onto something. Using new weapons, we were disturbing the enemy. Nontraditional venues were helping ensure that we were reached our targeted audiences, especially the black community. Billboards were putting a face on the millions of babies being slaughtered. We were going to them, speaking a new radical language, presenting them with the facts about what was going on. We were going to upend the abortion rhetoric and start a real conversation about life.

Action Steps

1. **Seek** nontraditional resources to use to awaken your community about the population control agenda inherent in abortion.

2. **Host** a screening of *MAAFA 21*.

3. **Host** education seminars in your church, school, or neighborhood, and call on seasoned, black, pro-life advocates to help tell the message.

4. **Raise** money to put up pro-life billboards in your community.

5. **Pray** for divine intervention to end abortion in America.

Chapter 9: Incremental Step or Knockout Punch?

By this time, Georgia Right to Life had drafted their piece of legislation, House Bill 1155, and dropped it with the clerk's office. Representative Barry Loudermilk stepped up to be its spokesperson. He had impressed me in 2008 during our exchange with then-Speaker of the House, Glenn Richardson, concerning the Speaker's eugenics beliefs. Loudermilk refused to cover up the conversations he had had with the former speaker. When asked a direct question, he told the truth. Needless to say when he stepped up to carry the bill, I was overjoyed. I knew he would stand on his principles rather than bow to the political winds that were blowing some of his peers to and fro.

GRTL decided to bring national black leaders to Georgia to help introduce the bill to our legislators. Each year, the RTL organization hosts a legislative breakfast. It is at this breakfast that pro-life legislation is introduced and legislators are encouraged to support it. We carefully selected several leaders to help us tell the story: Pastor Walter Hoye from Oakland California, Dr. Johnny Hunter from Fayetteville, N.C., Dr. LaVerne Tolbert from Burbank, California, and Dr. Alveda King, daughter of A.D. King, niece of Martin Luther King, Jr. These leaders each graciously accepted the invitation to come.

Interestingly, just a few months before, Pastor Hoye had been released from the Oakland City jail. What was his crime? Standing in front of an abortion mill with a sign that said: "Jesus loves you. Let me help." Other sidewalk counselors witnessed to the abortion-minded every day and were able to do so without incident or arrest. What was it that made Pastor Hoye so different - different enough that Oakland passed a bubble law that said he had to be 100 feet away from persons entering and exiting the abortion mill? Pastor Hoye is black. That is the only difference. He is the only person that has been arrested under this new law. We wanted him to tell the legislators his experience because it was plain that race was a factor in his incarceration.

Another leader who accepted our invitation, Dr. Hunter, is a veteran in the fight for life. He has built an effective pro-life organization called Life Educational And Resource Network (LEARN). This is a vast network of pastors, doctors, lawyers, community leaders, and pro-life organizations who promote life through education, legislation, and service. We asked Dr. Hunter to discuss his outreach efforts through black churches and the success he has had in reaching the black community.

Another invitee, Dr. Tolbert, is a former Planned Parenthood board member. We needed her testimony concerning Planned Parenthood's strategy of targeting the black community. Finally, Dr. King, a former Georgia legislator herself, was asked to share why Priests for Life hired her to reach the black community.

GRTL was strategic not only in choosing its presenters, but also in choosing the legislators who were to attend the breakfast. We invited the usual pro-life legislators, but for the first time, we also extended an invitation to every member of the Congressional Black Caucus—even though only one or two of them claimed to be pro-life. And these two pro-life pastors had never taken the lead on the issue, offered legislation to impact it, or voted for pro-life legislation. So we thought it was high time they all get engaged and heard the message about the holocaust taking place right under their noses. As a result, we had more than the usual two black legislators at our breakfast.

Immediately following, Melvin Everson, one of two black Republicans in the statehouse that year, invited members of the Black Caucus to a "for us only" meeting with our pro-life panel of leaders. These events were historical. Georgia Right to Life had not been able, until this point, to penetrate the Black Caucus. And as it turned out, eight Black Caucus members came to the "for us" only meeting. Wow. We had the opportunity to present the facts and openly share our hearts in this closed-door meeting. I really believed we had knocked the ball out of the park, challenging them to come alongside us as we fought the battle.

By this time I had managed to present my message to both Clark Atlanta and Morris Brown students in Atlanta. I had also been to Brenau University, Gainesville College, and Mercer University. The Mercer University screening of *Maafa21* was quite interesting. There were some among the more than sixty students and professors in attendance who openly espoused the doctrines of population control and eugenics. I was amazed by the boldness of these folk, to openly state that abortion is a viable means of controlling births so that the earth would not be overpopulated! They showed no hesitance in parroting the population control message I had not realized until that meeting that the philosophy of population control is so ingrained in the culture that almost no one would question it. These students believed it was politically incorrect to do anything but promote it.

I had delivered my plea to the Clayton County Ministerial Alliance, the Forest Park Ministers Association, and the Southside Ministers Alliance to name a few. The word was getting around and now there were churches that were calling me to come and speak or to do a screening of *Maafa21*. I hosted a screening of the documentary at my own church, The Father's House, where more than 100 people attended. This was the first time that many who came had ever participated in an open discussion about abortion. Questions were welcomed and answered in an environment where women felt safe.

I was careful to make every screening interactive by including a panel discussion. There are so many images and ideas that assault the senses in this documentary, I felt the need to ensure time for viewers to process through what they had seen. There had to be time for the viewers to rightly assign the responsibility for what they were seeing, rather than falling into the age old trap of crying racism but not directing the cry toward those who were truly guilty of it. In addition, these screenings allowed us to showcase the resources that are available to help abortion-minded woman choose other options and educate the community on what assistance is available for women in crisis.

Regarding the latter, I typically try to have a representative from area crisis pregnancy centers, abortion healing ministries, adoption services and/or other pro-life groups present to discuss their programs and resources. There are many good programs offered in the pro-life community for mothers who choose life including free parenting classes, pregnancy counseling, adoption counseling, and in some areas of the country, even residential housing for single mothers. We make sure that those in attendance are not only aware of those programs, but have immediate access to the staff of those programs. I cannot tell you how many times we have heard the complaint that pro-lifers do not care about the children once they are born, so having these caring advocates and counselors present at the screenings goes a long way in dispelling that myth.

The pro-abortion community was now scrambling to respond to our well-coordinated attack against them. After our first press conference, they decided to host one of their own. SisterSong and their affiliated organizations came together to protest our so called "attack" on black women. When they were convening, I stood on the steps of the Georgia Capitol, the site of their event, observing. I saw one of the most heart breaking and chilling things.

When Georgia Right to Life and the Radiance Foundation held our many discussions concerning the campaign, one of the frequently discussed questions was the level of visibility of the GRTL organization. We knew the pro-abortion community would "play the race card" by calling attention to the mostly white organization, claiming they wanted to control black women. Because many blacks view abortion as a white issue, we had to decide how we were going to address the matter as well as the tendency of some to call Ryan and I betrayers of the race. We had to face the questions of whether we were nothing more than puppets of the white pro-life movement. It would have been negligent not to measure what our response would be when these kind of questions were raised.

So we decided that ultimately when asked, we would acknowledge the GRTL role in funding the billboards and promoting the legislation. But the communications would focus more on Operation Outrage than on GRTL. This way, Ryan and I could be a little more free to share our heart for life without getting side tracked on who is funding the message and why. It was as if we were warning people to get out of a burning building, and they were too concerned about the color of the flames to take action.

Furthermore, there were times during the campaign that some were uncomfortable when I spoke about abortions' devastation on "my people." They said it sounded like I only cared about what happened to black babies and not to any other race of children. They wanted my message to be more inclusive. But let me set the record straight. I care desperately for all babies. Abortion however, is depopulating the black community and we should all be shouting it from the rooftops!

Planned Parenthood on the other hand, decided to hide their involvement in the protests from the public. They obviously thought it best to push their black members out front on the issue rather than stand with them as GRTL chose to do with me. So on the day of the SisterSong event, there were several white Planned Parenthood advocates that came to distribute signs and other paraphernalia to the attendees. When the hour struck for the conference to begin, not one of these women were present or even near the event – in fact they were nowhere to be seen. It then appeared as though these black and Latina women had convened at SisterSong's behest with no involvement of the white leaders of Planned Parenthood.

This was the first time I was able to see, firsthand, the implementation of Planned Parenthood's Negro Project. This time, in addition to black pastors and political leaders, they put on display the black woman themselves.

I was even more heartbroken to see, however, that some of the black legislators who had attended our "for us only" meeting were now standing with these protestors, openly declaring their opposition to our bill. To me, it meant these legislators had overridden at least the facts and perhaps their consciences to support the tapestry of lies woven into abortionists' doctrines.

Representative Loudermilk had introduced the House bill to the world, while Pastor Hoye, and Drs. Hunter, Tolbert, and King openly celebrated the legislation as a step toward life for babies in the womb. Once again, very few media attended. By now, however, we were not daunted in our efforts. We expected God would breathe on this one, as He had the other, and our message would be heard in Georgia and throughout the nation.

We were right in our thinking, and overnight every major media outlet was contacting us for an interview. MSNBC called two separate times. The New York Times even asked to follow me around to "get the story." This was the second interview by the Times within one month. By now, Associated Press reporter Errin Haynes had filed her story, and local newspapers throughout the country had picked up the message of the billboards and legislation. Every genre of media was carrying the story. The impact of abortion on the black community was going out over the airwaves.

Action Steps

1. **Lobby** your legislator to not only vote for pro-life legislation, but to sponsor and actively support it.

2. **Host** training sessions on effective lobbying.

3. **Host** a lobby day at your state capitol to rally members around pro-life legislation.

4. **Pray** for divine intervention to end abortion in America.

Chapter 10: Legislation, Round 2

The Georgia legislative process relies on committee hearings not only to fact find, but to gather information from those who favor the legislation as well as those who do not. Citizens are also allowed to come and state their position on the matter being heard. The first step for House Bill 1155 was the assignment of the legislation to the Judiciary Non-Civil Committee that has twenty one members—seven Democrats and fourteen Republicans. The committee process is for closely scrutinizing a bill, which usually can't happen when the bill is presented on the House or Senate floor.

The Judiciary Non-Civil Committee was the logical committee for this bill because there were criminal provisions in it. HB 1155 would have made it a felony for a doctor to knowingly perform an abortion that was coerced or race/gender based. The natural assumption was that the Republicans would all vote for the bill when it reached them, but first it had to survive the subcommittee hearings.

We prepared our documentation on what we believed was a clear demonstration of the racial impact abortion has had. We began with Margaret Sanger's Negro Project and worked our way through the studies which show how clinics are based on race more than other factors such as access or economics. This included studies which showed an increase in the number of abortions performed on women in the Asian community – where the desire for boys rather than girls has infiltrated American culture. Putting race and gender on the table was bold. It had not been done this way before, and legislators immediately showed their discomfort with them being in the bill. In Soon I began to hear rumors that some legislators were calling the bill the "Black Baby Bill." I was deeply disturbed when I began to hear that some of my Republican brothers and sisters wanted race taken out of the bill, and that there were backroom exchanges where legislators furiously debated killing the bill entirely.

Most could not handle how we were showing that race was indeed a factor in abortion decisions. Snide comments were frequently heard – people wanted to know if we really thought black women or Asian women would go into the abortion clinic and state that they did not want their baby because of its race or gender. Of course this wasn't what we were saying. We weren't proposing a scenario where a black woman goes into a clinic saying she wants her abortion because her baby is black—that would be silly. But we had heard of cases where white women who had consensual sex with black men were forced by parents, the boyfriend, or others to abort their children. In fact, a young white woman who had that experience came forward to testify that her parents had forced her to abort her black baby.

What was particularly interesting about her testimony was that she had wanted her child, but her will was overrun. Abortionists have it set up so that minors all over America can get an abortion without parental consent. Planned Parenthood elevates young girls to woman status and declares that they have "a woman's right to choose." However, when this particular "woman" declared to all clinic workers in hearing distance that she wanted her child, she was told that her parents knew best as they sedated her and took her child's life. When she gave this testimony, even the most hardened of legislators shed a tear.

Finally the vote came. The subcommittee of Republicans and two Democrats voted to pass it onto full committee. But it wasn't without drama. One of the black caucus members who said he was pro-life voted to move the bill on—we think—but when the vote was initially taken, he abstained, indicating he did not understand what vote was being taken. One of the Democratic legislators sarcastically broke it down for him, assuming he was voting against the bill. But to the surprise of many there, especially the SisterSong representatives, he indicated it was his intent to vote for the bill's passage to full committee.

Despite its passage out of subcommittee, our Republican friends were not happy with the bill the way it was. They asked us to tone down the race "rhetoric." I kept hearing that even though it was clear how abortion disproportionally impacts the black community in Georgia, we could not escape the inherent racism in many of the legislators. They just did not want to talk about or acknowledge race in any way. Some actually feared it would backfire on the Republicans by looking like a racist bill instead of an anti-discrimination one.

I should concede here that in some ways they were right, but in other ways they were as wrong as could be. Since the signing of the Civil Rights Act of 1964, there has been erosion in our understanding of what racism is. There are many today, especially here in Atlanta, who believe any time a white person says something about a black person, especially a black Democrat, even if it is true, it is racism. So the fear that white legislators could be labeled racist for supporting this bill was a legitimate fear. After all, they had seen many white politicians and public figures in similar situations have their careers destroyed by the backlash from black Democrats.

On the other hand, there was a measure of racism being acted out to the glee of the pro-aborts and dismay of pro-lifers. We had clearly laid out all the parameters that point to race as a factor in abortion: the 1974 study that revealed race was a factor in the location of birth control clinics (Family Planning Services and the Distribution of Black Americans), Margaret Sanger's letter to Dr. C. J. Gamble explaining the Negro Project, the facts as presented in *Maafa21*, etc. However, many legislators, blacks and whites alike, decided to ignore these facts.

The backroom discussions about the "Black Baby Bill" continued. It seemed like many of the legislators wanted to keep abortion unrestrained, should they ever have to face the situation of a black man impregnating one of their daughters. The whisper campaign in the halls of the Capitol applauded the efforts of those attempting to block the passage of this legislation. At the same time, the black legislators had already pledged themselves to the largesse of Planned Parenthood and other abortion providers. They too were unwilling to restrain the hand of the abortionist. Thus, they were allowing unborn babies to be sacrificed on the altar of political expediency.

So we had to adjust our comments for the full committee in a way that would de-emphasize race and highlight the other provisions in the bill such as coercion. It was not hard to make this shift since there are reports that tell us coercion is a factor in more than 64% of abortions.[36] Pastors, parents, teachers, husbands, boyfriends, and others are reported to force abortions on women again and again. It still sticks in my craw, however, that we had to downplay the race factor in order to appease Republicans, the party founded to end slavery.[37]

The very week of the hearings on the bill, The Economist magazine released a shocking statement on its front page report: "Gendercide, Killed, Aborted or Neglected, at least 100m girls have disappeared—and the number is rising."[38] Such fabulous timing! We led with this article and others that so clearly illustrated coercion and gendercide.

Shenanigans started going on during the hearing. Remember the Black Caucus member who had voted to allow the bill out of subcommittee? He was not free to vote his conscience this time. Every five to ten minutes, the lead Democrat assigned to rein him in, pulled him out of the hearing and into the hallway in what was a clear effort to corral him into voting their way. He was so skittish that by the end of the hearing, he threw his hands in the air refusing to hear another word from anyone – pro-life or pro-abortion. Rather than voting his convictions, he abstained, unwilling to tolerate another moment of harassment from his peers to vote against his conscience.

Up until this point, my biggest beef with my brothers and sisters in the pro-life movement had been our unwillingness to stand together for the good of the movement. During the civil rights demonstrations, those participating in the Freedom Rides and sit-ins were instructed to keep rank under all circumstances. Alveda King tells a story about the time she broke rank while trying to help a friend that went down under the onslaught of the police. She was arrested and her dad, A. D. King, let her stay in jail all night. She had to learn not to break rank. I had hoped the commitment to the unborn would be as strong as the commitment in civil rights movement, but I learned that many who claim they are committed to life, are not. Instead, they are committed to getting elected. They cannot do so without the support of the pro-choice community so they fold when the going gets tough.

[36] http://www.theunchoice.com/whateveryamerican.htm

[37] http://www.gop.com/our-party/our-history/

[38] http://www.economist.com/node/15606229

Even some who allegedly committed their political careers to stand with us, ran faster than roaches when the light was turned on. Even though we had soft-pedaled the racial issue and focused on coercion, there were still some Republicans who hoped to kill the bill. It didn't help that as the hearing continued, Democrats routinely objected to every proposition that was put forth by Republicans. Legislators were in and out of the room as those present spoke for and against the bill. Finally, it was time to vote.

There was one Republican legislator whose vote we were especially concerned about. She had a tendency to be erratic and was clearly not a friend of life. So we prayed. Specifically, we asked for confusion of language of any who would continue speaking against the bill. As expected, our Republican friend began a rant against the bill and moved to table it. When her motion was defeated, she began to whirl around and around in a circle and stomp her foot! Turning beet red, she became so frustrated she could not speak – and she did not vote. At all. There was no abstaining, no thumbs up, or down. She did not vote at all. The bill passed out of committee and was slated to go on to the Rules Committee, by a margin of just one vote.

An even more peculiar thing was to happen at the conclusion of the hearing. It was the response of a Black Caucus member to one of the pro-abortion advocates. As the advocate laid her head upon the legislator's breast in sorrow, I heard the legislator say, "Hold your head up baby. God is still in control." I was stunned. I could not believe that this legislator was invoking God in their pro-abortion debate. At least not the God I serve. The Bible tells us that the shedding of innocent blood is one of the seven things God hates, and that God knit us together in our mother's womb. So I could not imagine anyone in the pro-abortion arena truly believing that the God of the universe, the one and only wise God, would endorse the heinous practice of abortion. However, listening to this Black Caucus member attempting to encourage this woman, I was deeply saddened and burdened because I know they did believe God was on their side.

Nevertheless, our victory was particularly savory because we had really dodged a time constraint bullet. If a bill has not been voted on, in either house, by the 30th legislative day of the session, it faces certain death. We would have been heart-broken if a long, hard fought committee-level victory came too late to meet this crucial deadline. Well, we got our vote with a little over two weeks to spare.

The next steps of the legislative process were for the bill to go to the Rules Committee and then onto the floor of the House for the final vote. We thought it would be easy to get the bill through the Rules Committee, especially since the GRTL lobbyist had dubbed the chair of that committee "USDA prime" on pro-life issues. Our celebration proved premature because suddenly we were hearing that the Speaker of the House had the bill recommitted – sent back to committee. We thought we could get answers about this move from the bill's sponsor, Representative Loudermilk, but even he was not notified about this development. In fact, none of our usual contacts, including the Chair of the Non-Judiciary Committee was able to provide insight about the bill's status and the Speaker's objections to it. We were in the dark, and that darkness was growing and spreading, infecting the entire process.

It was not until the following week that we were told the Speaker of the House had problems with some of the language in the bill. He believed the definition of coercion was too broad and needed to be more narrowly explained. We were told he had volunteered his legal counsel to work with the author and sponsor of the bill to correct the deficient language. We cautiously rejoiced. Cautiously because we had begun to hear that the Speaker was longtime friends with an attorney everyone knew had been the leading lobbyist for Planned Parenthood. And the unofficial report was that she was frequently seen in and out of the Speaker's office. Some said she had already struck a deal with the Speaker and all our efforts were for naught. We didn't have all the facts so we hoped for the best.

Never one to sit doing nothing, I continued my outreach efforts in hopes of enlisting more blacks in the fight. I arranged more screenings of *Maafa21*, visited area colleges and universities, and began to seek more endorsements of the bill. The clock continued to tick and time was running out for the bill. The author of the bill, along with the sponsor, was meeting with the Speaker's counsel on a continuing basis in an attempt to tighten the language. When there was nothing left to tighten, the bill languished in the Speaker's hands and was not placed on the calendar for a vote on the changes. Finally, we decided to find a sponsor for the bill in the Senate in order to ensure the bill did not die because it was not passed before crossover day.

Senator Chip Pearson (R-Dawsonville) was delighted to lead the charge in the Senate so the bill was sent to the clerk of the Senate and assigned a number. In effect, we were no longer working toward passing House Bill 1155; we were now pushing for Senate Bill 529. Within days of being dropped, we had a committee hearing where once again the facts were given. Joining the team was an attorney, Jonathan Crumbly, who masterfully presented the facts for our side. He was able to field the legal questions the members had and clarify concerns that arose. The version of the bill submitted to the Senate also included all language changes recommended by the counsel for the Speaker of the House. From start to finish, the bill was sent to the floor of the Senate in record time.

Lines were drawn and the Democrats put forth their best arguments against the bill. One pleasant surprise was the allies we picked up when some black Senators offended the white Senators—the black Senators told the white Senators that they (as whites) could not know how to help a black child. This was a foot-in-the-mouth moment because some of those white Senators had adopted a black child or had family members who had. While they had not been inclined to vote with us before, they now were because they were so outraged by those remarks.

There was one black Democrat Senator who we supremely hoped would vote with us. He is a pastor who proclaims himself pro-life and gave a speech about his sister choosing life for her child, whom the doctors had said would be born with disabilities, and was. The baby died not too long after birth, but they loved her and took care of her even though she was disabled.

But this pastor abstained from voting because he said legislation needed to address children who are living equally to those in the womb. Now I am not at all clear on how someone can say the killing of a baby in the womb is permissible because there is not sufficient legislation to address concerns of other children who have been born. This is especially perplexing since none of these same legislators sponsored bills that would address the very concerns they were outlining! There are of course many circumstances our children are forced to face, often before they are mature enough to handle life. But the killing of a child before they even have a chance at life can never be an acceptable course of action. This kind of excuse can be lumped into the larger complaint that pro-life advocates don't do enough for the mothers who choose life, which is false as we discussed already. It is a common tactic used by abortion defenders.

Another common ruse, used by Georgia's black legislators to avoid the question of abortion's impact on the black community, is saying that Republicans won't support legislation sponsored by black legislators. I had one legislator to tell me he would support SB529 if I supported legislation to place a moratorium on the death penalty. He spoke about the numbers of inmates who were on death row and had been released because DNA demonstrated they were not the perpetrator of the crime. I immediately agreed that if he sponsored a bill to put a moratorium on the death penalty, I would lobby the Republicans to support it. I even suggested he add to such legislation by proposing that the state test every death row inmates' DNA if it is available. That way, if there were any inmates who were innocent, this legislation would see their immediate release on the state's terms.

This same legislator first made the death penalty argument to me in 2008. I said the same thing to him each time he proposed the moratorium. I have yet to see any piece of legislation this representative or any other black caucus member offered to address this concern. They simply talk. They never take action to do anything about it, or any other issues plaguing the black community. It is smoke and mirrors.

So House Bill 1155 became Senate Bill 529, and it passed in record time along party lines, making its way through committee hearings and floor debates in time to cross back over to the House. We could now return to the House side and renew our efforts to get the bill out of committee and onto the floor of the House. This time when the bill was assigned to committee, it did not go back to the Judiciary Non- Civil Committee.   Instead, it was assigned to the "committee from hell."

"Committee from hell," what is that, you ask? That this the title the Vice Chair gave to the Judiciary Committee. This committee is not known to pass or support legislation that addresses pro-life issues, and they are known to put any such bill through the paces to find any viable means of stopping it. We braced ourselves for what we knew was going to be an epic fight.

Action Steps

1. **Identify** and support pro-life legislation in your state.

2. **Learn** the Legislative process.

3. **Attend** hearings and comment on the legislation.

4. **Lobby** your legislators on the legislation.

5. **Pray** God will end the scourge of abortion in America.

Chapter 11. The Cost of Partisanship

What was particularly interesting during this time of back and forth, was the announcement by the pro-abortion folk that if this bill passed in Georgia it would change the face of abortion in the nation. Everyone was calling in every favor they had, to stop it in its tracks. The Democrats were being held to their allegiance to Planned Parenthood and other abortion providers. Every screw that could be tightened was being tightened. They were shamelessly pulling legislators out of the committee hearings, off the floor, and catching them in the corridors to ensure they stood firm on their commitments to the abortion agenda. Oh that the Republicans were as committed to life!

In the hands of the committee from hell, the bill was not assigned to a subcommittee hearing. The first hearing of the full committee allowed anyone who wanted to speak, time to speak. We were told that statements could be made and accepted, but no vote would be taken that day. Each side was allowed time to present their information and once submitted, the committee would adjourn. We brought back the same information and witnesses who had presented to the Civil Non-Judiciary Committee, including the young lady whose parents threatened to put her on the street if she did not abort her black child.

Some of the pro-abortion Black Caucus members questioned the statement provided by the young woman, wanting to know why neither the father of the child nor the parents had been prosecuted for coercion. They expressed dismay that those who coerced the young woman were not being held accountable or prosecuted. And they demanded that provisions be placed in our bill to hold the mother accountable for terminating the child, if indeed the abortion was based on race or gender. They also insisted there were already laws on the books to prosecute coercion. Our bill, they said, was not needed.

All of this was sleight of hand, completely ignoring the official stance Planned Parenthood and others take towards vulnerable girls considering abortion. Planned Parenthood workers, for example, have been caught on video counseling young girls on how to keep the fact that their sexual partner is an adult, secret. They actually try to persuade young girls to get abortions, not hold them accountable for why they're seeking it. Nor do they care anything about coercion, even when they witness it. They are trained to call the girls "young women," no matter what their age. They tell her she has the right to "choose" unless her choice is to keep the child, in which case they try to persuade her that the skeptical adults in her life are right to advise her to abort. And the boys are always "young men," even if they aren't.

So this song and dance the Georgia legislators were doing completely misrepresented abortion providers. Providers are always in the tank for a young girl to have an abortion, coercion or not. They supply their own coercion! The fact is, our bill would have helped this woman who testified, but those who opposed our bill would have enabled more to follow in her footsteps.

But the street fight had just begun. As tedious as it was, Georgia Right to Life had continued to lobby this whole time, walking the corridors and urging Republicans to stay strong in the fight. I myself had been working behind the scenes to create a coalition that would speak publicly for life. It was at this hearing that the results of my labors were published.

Four significant leaders had written letters urging the passage of Senate Bill 529. It has been well known in pro-life circles that the president of the Georgia NAACP, Ed Dubose, is pro-life. In fact, the Georgia NAACP passed a resolution in 2007 to reduce the number of young black Americans lost to abortion. Dubose accepted our invitation to join us in calling on the Speaker to allow the bill to get to the floor of the House. Also, the president of the Georgia Southern Christian Leadership Conference (SCLC), Samuel Mosteller, accepted the same invitation. Bishop Wellington Boone of the Fellowship of International Churches, and Dr. Creflo Dollar of World Changers Ministry joined these leaders in calling on the Speaker to allow the bill out of committee. This coalition was historic, stunning the members of the Black Caucus to silence that day.

In response, there were a number of physicians lined up to testify for the pro-abortion side. It is interesting to note that not one of these physicians were abortionists. Some were not even OB-GYN's! They very plaintively laid out a case that if Senate Bill 529 passed, it would impede their ability to provide family planning counseling to their patients. Each ignored, or were not aware of, the safety net provision in the bill which would have exempted them from prosecution if they followed the procedure outlined. At the conclusion of all the testimony, the committee adjourned and we were left wondering what next.

As all of this excitement was going on, I was praying and asking God for His divine intervention to block all the craziness of the legislators. I truly believed I had a promise from God that the bill would also pass the "committee from hell" unscathed, with no amendments. When I told my co-laborers of the promise, they all looked at me as if I had antennae growing from my head, and they patronizingly agreed – more to get me to shut up than anything else. But I was unmoved by their lack of belief and continued trusting God that what He had revealed to me was true.

There was one unexpected hiccup in the middle of the process. When I ran for Congress, there was a lady that came to work on my campaign all the way from Paulding County, which was far from where I lived. She drove me to many of the meetings and debates which were scheduled around the district. She also held a fundraiser for me to get the much-needed funds to get my message out and she recruited workers to join the campaign in various capacities. Needless to say, she and I became dear friends, and that friendship has survived many a political challenge over the years. When the word came that her mother had passed away, I knew there was no way that I could not go to the funeral to pay my respects. But the funeral was on the same day "committee from hell" scheduled the vote on our bill. I was torn. I needed to go to the funeral at 2:00, but I needed to go to the committee hearing at 3:00. And the funeral was far from the Capitol where the hearing was to be held. I went to the funeral.

Let me just say, I had never been to a funeral that was that short. Literally thirty minutes from arrival, the funeral was over. I was back in my car by 2:35pm, waiting for the cars to leave. That was divine intervention! When I arrived at the Capitol, I ran to the hearing room only to find I could not get in. There was standing room only and one of the largest men in the hearing was standing in front of the door, preventing another soul from getting in. As I looked through the door, I could not tell how it was going. All the pro-lifers had their best poker faces on, as did the pro-aborts. So I began to pace the hall in front of the room, praying and asking God to shift the environment to favor the babies.

I would periodically stop and look in, trying to see how it was going. Again and again, I prayed and looked into the room, looked into the room and prayed. Finally, the GRTL lobbyist looked out and when he saw me, drew his finger across his throat. Our bill was being butchered. This time, rather than pacing, I found an empty room and cried out to God with all that was in me, asking him to shift the hearing in our favor. When I went back to the hearing room, many in the room began to stream out and suddenly I was able to get into the room and find a seat.

The debate was fierce. A substitute bill had been introduced and the committee seemed inclined to pass it. Back and forth they went until the vote was taken. The substitute bill passed. I prayed some more, unwilling to be moved from the promise I believed God had given me. As soon as the substitute passed, a Republican legislator, Mark Hatfield, made a motion to table it. One of the lead black Democrats fighting the bill was enraged, believing the motion to table was out of order. He called the parliamentary question. The parliamentarian ruled the motion in order. A vote was taken and the motion to table passed.

Everyone, including the Democrat protester, wondered what was next. The committee Chair announced it was time to vote on SB529 as it had been presented to the committee. "No, no," the Democrat yelled, "that is out of order!" The parliamentary question was again called. The parliamentarian again ruled the vote in order. A vote was taken. SB529 passed, with no amendments or changes. Even the Republicans whom I thought would vote against it, voted for it. Surprise, surprise!!

Hurray, praise God, we succeeded. The bill would now go to the floor of the House. We would prevail and babies and women would be protected from coercion, race and gender discrimination in Georgia.

Well, not so much. Once again the Speaker of the House pulled the bill, stopped it in its tracks in the Rules Committee, and refused to let it out onto the floor. By now the media had gotten wind of the battle and they were being told by both sides that if the bill were allowed to get to the floor, it would pass. Reporters were running back and forth between both camps, looking for the next headline, the next story. The tension was so thick you could have cut it with a knife.

In the midst of the action, a debate had been scheduled between me and the representative from SisterSong, Heidi Williamson. It was to be held in the heart of black Atlanta, at the Sweet Auburn Bistro on Auburn Avenue. The moderator was Maynard Eaton, an award winning journalist. He was to interview Heidi Williamson and me, raising questions related to the bill and the billboards. The room was packed, again standing room only. Even those outside the room, seated at the bar and in the second dining room, were closely listening.

Back and forth we went, answering question after question until the last one, when Heidi dropped a bombshell. She said, "We are working to make sure Senate Bill 529 is defeated by *sine die* [without any future date being designated for resumption]." She continued, "It is not over literally until it is over. While it did pass out of committee, there are no guarantees it will go to the floor. The Speaker has the discretion to hold it, send it back, and do whatever he likes. We are exercising all of our resources to make sure it does not make it out."

I could not get back to our legislators fast enough to get an update. Why was Heidi so confident the bill would prohibited from the floor? What did she know that we did not know? No matter who I questioned about this, no one seemed to know what she was talking about. This time I had no promise from God. This time I was not confident of the outcome. While shenanigans had been afoot the entire time, they were now kicked up to another level. The woman known as the leading lobbyist for abortion proponents now had her Cheshire cat grin on each time any one of us encountered her. Her walk became a glide, queenly signaling she knew something we didn't.

So we did the only thing we could do. We called for reinforcements. Governor Huckabee was asked to assist us in activating the pro-life base. He called a number of Georgia districts and urged voters to call their Representative, asking them to tell the Speaker to allow the bill to get to the floor. GRTL also asked some prominent Republican Congressmen and other respected leaders to call upon the Speaker and ask him to let the bill out of committee. The nation's eyes were on Georgia to see how this would turn out.

Still, the pro-abortion forces seemed to have the upper hand. They appeared more and more confident as the end of the legislative session approached. In all honesty, my confidence was waning. The unknown factor in this drama was the Speaker. No one was able to read him, and no one knew his motive for blocking the bill. Sure, Georgia Right to Life had a lapse in judgment when it endorsed a former chapter president over him when he ran for his seat. But that was ten years before, and I refused to believe he was stopping the bill because of a 10-year-old wound. After all, he was now the leader of the House of Representatives in the state of Georgia. Surely his motive could not be that petty. He had not sought the GRTL endorsement since that time but had repeatedly characterized himself as pro-life. When he spoke before conservatives he had all the right language, even calling on the name of the Lord. Surely we could trust that he was indeed pro-life as he held himself out to be.

At this point I still had faith that those calling themselves pro-life would live up to their moniker. I still believed that it was more than a political tool to get elected. I thought each of them would look at the bill from the perspective of the community, and from the women that would be helped. This bill ensured that the abortion clinic became the last line of safety for the woman being forced to kill her child. It brought a measure of accountability to ensure no child died because it was the "wrong" gender or race. I still had problems understanding how the Black Caucus and others could openly fight a bill that afforded babies this protection. It was basic anti-discrimination law, similar to acts that had passed for transportation, employment, and other circles—perfectly legal. I was wrestling with these thoughts and praying that God would continue to "meddle" in the affairs of men by letting this bill pass.

All too soon, day forty arrived. After this day, the lobbying was done. If the bill did not make it to the floor now, it was dead for the year. Of course, day forty felt like the longest day ever. It seemed to drag by. As the GRTL lobbyist and President pressured the caucus to pressure the Speaker, it seemed we were getting further and further away from achieving the goal we had fought so hard for. Back and forth the legislators went between the Speaker, his counsel and the caucus - each report that came back to us was more negative than the one before it. In the last hour before the declaration of sine die, the die was cast and we knew our fight for this session was done. The nail resounded when the Speaker's Counsel was seen with lobbyists from the pro-abortion community allegedly rewriting SB529. Heidi's prediction was true. The Speaker did not allow our bill to go to the floor for a vote.

When the dust settled, I was confused. The legislative process had been followed meticulously. Each committee hearing allowed for dissent and comment, and the hearing process had been carried out to the letter. I did not understand then, and cannot understand now, how one man could violate the integrity of the process and it be allowed to stand. Moreover, there was no outrage that SB529 died an ignoble death at the hands of a Republican. I did not hear any moral outcry that a Republican Speaker of the House had sided openly with the abortion industry, while at the same time saying he was pro-life. The agents of abortion made it clear they had formed a coalition with the Speaker, but there was no step that could be taken to hold him accountable. That I do not understand.

Never had it been clearer, that at that moment, those in the pro-life movement were mistaken in thinking "Republican" was synonymous with "Christian" or "conservative." Our blind trust in those Republicans to do the right thing had been betrayed. For 39 years, the pro-life movement had searched for a piece of legislation that would be a direct challenge to Roe v. Wade. In SB529, there was not only a direct challenge, but there were provisions to help women that had been harmed by an abortionist. All involved, on both sides of the bill, acknowledged that SB529 would meet the objective of challenging Roe, yet the Speaker was allowed to say he did not want to do so. And because he did not want to, he was allowed to kill the bill.

Still, there was some good news to celebrate. For a very long time, few if any blacks openly talked about abortion. Because of our "Endangered Species" campaign though, women all over America were now discussing abortion. Hundreds if not thousands of women were talking about their own experiences in the abortion mill. Information was getting out that the so-called "safe, legal abortion" was not so safe after all. Women were still dying, except at the hands of the licensed abortionist rather than the back alley butcher. Opportunities had opened up to discuss the link between breast cancer and abortion, and the extreme premature birth rate now found among women who have had an induced abortion.

A spotlight was also now shining on the little known fact that 55 million abortions were not committed on 55 million different women. More than 50% of abortions have been performed on women who have had an abortion previously. This is one of the documented signs of post- abortion syndrome. Talk shows now had women calling in, telling of their own five or more abortions, or the five or more abortions their friends had. Ritual abortion and abortion as birth control were now on the radar.

Men were also given an opportunity to voice their opposition to the killing of their children. Many came forward to relate the story of how they had wanted their baby but were overruled by the mother's "right to choose." Facts spread regarding the level of coercion that is often involved in the decision to abort. Woman after woman was now free to relate her own story about parents, partners, and others applying pressure to abort. New alliances had been formed, and doors were now open to begin cementing future alliances. There would be more action regarding abortion in Georgia. There was good news indeed.

Most importantly, a new vocabulary was starting to frame the debate. The civil right of the child to be born was entering conversations around the country. The inhuman term "fetus" was being replaced with more accurate nouns to name who is in the mother's womb—"child" and "baby." Discussions were changing to include the paramount right of the child to be born. But there was another shift that was a little surprising.

Action Steps

1. **Identify** the position of your legislator on the life issue.

2. **Encourage** him or her to adopt/promote ground breaking legislation such as SB529.

3. **Groom** pro-life candidates to replace those in your state that refuse to stay true to pro-life principles above all else.

4. **Pray** that God will end the scourge of abortion in America.

Chapter 12 The Betrayal

There is a scene in the movie *Braveheart* when William Wallace is wrestling with The Bruce and he rips the helmet off as he is preparing to slit his throat. When he sees that his adversary is the Bruce, Wallace is frozen into inaction, stunned by the betrayal of the leader he thought was fighting for the people of Scotland. The range of emotion that crosses his face leaves him unable to kill the Bruce and vulnerable to the King's army that is coming over the ridge. That is how I felt when I learned of the betrayal of the Congressional Black Caucus.

On May 10, 2012, there was a briefing hosted by the Congressional Black Caucus and Pro-Choice Caucus on Capitol Hill. Several "undercover" pro-life supporters were able to attend and get the action plan that was laid out in the meeting. Those in attendance absolutely acknowledged the population control agenda of the abortion industry, agreeing that the numbers reported by members of the pro-life community are accurate.

Congresswoman Barbara Lee who represents California's 9th district, not only acknowledged the genocidal impact of abortion on the black community, but was heard saying it was her mission to help fulfill the population control agenda, saying something to the effect that there were still more black teenagers than white. She, along with other Congressional members, were very proud to discuss a strategy that included framing the issue as black women's "lack of access" to quality healthcare and education, rather than genocide as so many black pro-life abolitionists discuss.

The presenters acknowledged that the numbers of abortions performed on black women is disproportionately higher than on other ethnic groups. In fact, it has been reported that they agreed that the numbers cited by the pro-life community are true. Yet, these elected officials were very comfortable in presenting their tactics and strategies to deflect the conversation onto topics of reproductive justice and access to reproductive healthcare instead of the genocidal impact of abortion on blacks.

It was clear that these women, most of whom are black, understood they were promoting a population control agenda. Their drive to keep abortion on demand at any stage of the child's development legal, overrode any consideration of a more insidious plan to control the black birth rate through abortion. I had encountered this abortion-at-all-costs attitude earlier in my work, when I came face to face with the implementation of eugenics policy in the state of Georgia.

I saw first-hand how, birthed from the loins of population control enthusiasts, pro-aborts cloaked abortion in a web of deception. I saw how they framed the discussion in terms of women's rights and in recent days, reproductive justice. And what happens is, those who support abortion periodically come together to lay out the game plan for their foot soldiers so that each knows what to say and when to say it. Exposing this deception is one of the most difficult tasks of the pro-life movement because it is so deeply imbedded in the culture, that even pro-lifers cannot agree on steps to expose it. Some fear the outcome while others do not recognize it.

Here's what I saw. To prepare their foot soldiers, they enumerated talking points such as:

- Every community should have access to quality healthcare.

- Cite historical disparities whenever the pro-life community refers to the numbers of abortions on black women. Call for an end to the disparities.

- Challenge the other side to defend why they are contributing to racial disparities, i.e. "Why do you want to make the situation worse?"

- Move the discussion to the idea of trusting black women to make decisions for themselves.

- Circumstances really matter in the abortion discussion, so bring the audience to the idea of self-determination, not trying to second-guess women.

- Black women are more religious, but 37% of black women believe abortion should be available for any reason, at all stages of pregnancy. Most black women are in the middle.
- Attitudes on abortion are not swayable based on religion. Don't be afraid of the religious message because black women will say God gave them choice.[39]

They were also coaching their participants to give elevator speeches like this one:

"Every community in America should have access to quality healthcare including family planning services. Unfortunately, African American communities have historically suffered from substandard healthcare, family planning and education all of which contribute to unintended pregnancies, infant maternal deaths, and other serious health issues. So we need to end the historical and ongoing racial disparities in reproductive care that harm our community. When it comes to reproductive health and abortion we should respect the decisions made by black women because we can't know all the personal and medical reasons that went into every person's decision to have an abortion."[40]

Attendees were told to build the case by putting in a lot of healthcare and reproductive health care verbiage into the message before they get to abortion. The shortened version of the elevator pitch they were told to say was, "We need to end the historical and ongoing disparities in healthcare for African Americans that lead to unintended pregnancies and other serious health issues."

In order to refute the message of the pro-life billboards, attendees were told to turn the message back on pro-lifers by stating that the killing or endangering is really happening "by substandard healthcare and the lack of good education."[41] They were told to shift, always, the discussion toward education and substandard healthcare.

At the conclusion of the briefing, one of the conveners took great care to thank the funding sources that had given so generously in support of the forum: the Ford and Irving Harris

[39] http://www.jillstanek.com/2012/05/inside-congressional-caucus-briefing-on-how-to-block-pro-life-gains-in-black-community/

[40] http://www.jillstanek.com/?s=day+gardner

[41] http://www.guttmacher.org/pubs/fb_induced_abortion.html

Foundations. These organizations are among America's elite that have kept the eugenics movement alive and well in this nation. The Ford Foundation has a long history with the birth control and later abortion movement having been a part of the movement since its inception.

Action Steps

1. **Take** care to no longer use the terminology of the abortion industry.

2. **Speak** of the issue in Biblical terms.

3. **Find** resources in your community that provide post-abortion recovery services that you can refer post-abortive women to.

4. **Utilize** resources such as *Blood Money*, *Maafa 21*, and other documentaries that can help you re-frame the debate in life terms.

5. **Pray** that God will end the scourge of abortion in America.

Chapter 13: Republicans - Friends or Foes ?

In the forty years since the legalization of abortion in 1973, there have been five Republican and three Democrat Presidents. *Roe v. Wade* was decided when Richard Nixon, a Republican, was president. He not only supported it, but signed the first family planning legislation—thereby launching the population control agenda that has been steeped in the industry since its inception.

What about Congress? At least three of the five Republican presidencies were undergirded with a Republican Senate and/or House for part, if not all, of their terms. During this same time period, Republican presidents appointed, and the Congress confirmed, twelve of the sixteen Supreme Court Justices appointed between 1969 and 2010. Most people thought these appointments would ensure the overturn of *Roe v. Wade*, but they haven't. We have had more than 55 million babies die at the abortionist's hands—more than 1.2 million babies per year since 1977—and it is hard to see any progress forthcoming at the federal level.

What about the local level? Around the country, states have more Republican governors than ever before. Also, the number of Republican-led state Houses has increased, giving Republicans more leverage than ever. Yet, the abortion industry has enjoyed hands-off practices for most if not all of the past forty years. Even states that have enacted solid pro-life legislation such as Georgia have taken a step back and turned a blind eye to laws on the books.

We must conclude that putting on the uniform of the Republican Party has served no purpose other than getting candidates elected. Once elected, these candidates who pledged to show leadership, and even pledged to end abortion, become a part of the political establishment repeatedly allowing abortionists to operate at the edge or outside the law.

In 2010, for example, the nation was horrified to hear about Kermit Gosnell and his house of horrors in Philadelphia.[42] After almost forty years of running a multi-million dollar abortion practice with his wife, mainly for poor, immigrant, and minority women, he was finally arrested for murder and fraudulent and grotesque malpractice. Despite years of complaints from physicians, patients, and others, the state turned a blind eye and allowed Gosnell to operate each and every day, injuring women, murdering babies, and butchering them. He induced labor, delivered live babies, and then snipped their spinal cords with scissors. Only when one of his patients died from a botched abortion did the Commonwealth move to clean up abortion in that state. Time will tell if they really cleaned it up.

What about Georgia, the state where I live? Since 1973, 1,206,940 babies have died by abortion. For most of those years, the state was led by Democrat governors and legislators who proudly supported and promoted abortion. When Sonny Perdue rode in on the wave of pro-life and other votes, suddenly for the first time in more than 180 years, a Republican was leading the state. Quickly the Senate and House followed suit, with more Republicans being elected or Democrats switching party. Good news for the pro-life community right? Not so much. The horror that is abortion in Georgia is still unfolding every day.

Meanwhile, as was the case in Pennsylvania, there is a trail of injured women all across the state. Reports of squalid conditions, terrorized women, and passing infections through dirty instruments are common here. Calling state agencies such as the Department of Community Health or Department of Public health to get answers to the simplest of questions has become a morass of lawyers, dragging the questioners into the darkness that is abortion in this state. Though the process of filing complaints against abortionists is quite easy, Georgia has taken no steps to rein in the renegade abortionist when violations are found.

As a result, patients in Georgia are reporting they have bacterial infections, experience sepsis in incomplete abortions, and perforated bowels and uterus. Some abortion centers violate the

[42]http://articles.nydailynews.com/2011-01-19/news/27088082_1_abortion-clinic-late-term-abortions-aborted-fetuses

laws of Georgia every day by operating on the second floor without an elevator, allowing unlicensed staff to administer anesthesia and/or sonograms, and failing to escort patients as required by waivers. There are other violations we cannot even chronicle because the information is being hidden by both the State and the abortionists. The abortion industry is filled with dark, dirty secrets.

These are only going to grow. In 2008, President-elect Obama was provided a transition plan titled, "Advancing Reproductive Rights and Health in a New Administration." In that plan, those who supported abortion laid out their diabolical agenda for imbedding abortion more deeply in the culture. In President Obama, they found their chiefest ally as he implemented most, if not all, of the requests made. (They knew he would—he had already voted for the most radical anti-life legislation as a Congressman, which denied life-saving care to babies who survived a botched abortion!)

Now upmost of 90% of African-American voters gave their votes to the president in 2008 and in 2012. But he and the Congressional Black Caucus betrayed those who voted for them by granting the requests of the number one killer of African-Americans. They promoted the lies that abortion is safe, a matter of reproductive health. They didn't protect those who elected them, as was their responsibility, but instead did them a gross injustice.

After President Obama's reelection in 2012, instead of providing the president with a shopping list of tasks as they did in 2008, Planned Parenthood took off the rhetorical cloak in which they shrouded their agenda. So confident that abortion is here to stay, within a day of the election, the president of Planned Parenthood, Cecile Richards, issued an invitation to the Republicans to return to their family planning roots. She said: "A lot of Republicans used to support family planning, and Richard Nixon signed that first federal planning program into law. There's a clear pathway to [win back women's support], and it's to listen to the middle of their party instead of the extreme fringe."[43]

[43] http://www.huffingtonpost.com/2012/11/07/cecile-richards-planned-parenthood-election_n_2089855.html

Ms. Richards candidly praised Richard Nixon, who was a racist president and supported abortion as a means of controlling black births. Here are just a few of his sentiments: [44]

- "A majority of people in Colorado voted for **abortion**. I think a majority of people in Michigan are for **abortion**. I think in both cases, well, certainly in Michigan they will vote for it [**abortion**] because they think that what's going to be **aborted** generally are the little **black bastards**.

- "…as I told you – we talked about it earlier – that a hell of a lot people want to control the **Negro bastards**."

- "…you know what we are talking about –**population control**."

Clearly, while the Republican Party platform has an official pro-life statement, Republican affiliation is not the key to pro-life victory. It provides no security that the unborn will be stalwartly defended and protected. Perhaps we need a new strategy that will rip open the bloated and blood- filled belly of the abortion industry. Instead of relying on electing Republicans, the time has come for ferreting out and supporting true leadership on the question of life. Forty years of abortion and five Republican presidents clearly tells us to end the insanity of doing the same thing but expecting a different result.

---

[44] White House Tape 700/10 — Monday, April 3rd, 1972. Republican President Richard Milhous Nixon was the 37th President of the United States, serving from 1969 to 1974.

Action Steps

1. **Groom** candidates to run for elected office and who will work to end abortion in America.

2. **Question** existing legislators about their stance on abortion. Are they Nixon Republicans or Lincoln Republicans?

3. **Urge** lawmakers to show leadership and end abortion in America.

4. **Pray** for God to end the scourge of abortion in America.

Chapter 14: Abortion Must End

There are some words that once spoken, cause a reaction. "Abortion" is one of those words. Simply speaking the word out loud is cause enough for debate. Within moments of it being uttered, the rhetoric begins to fly with the rapidity of firing an AK-47. Those for abortion fire off their arguments in pro-abortion language, and those against abortion fire off their arguments in pro-life language.

Within nanoseconds, the conversation is no longer about abortion but morphs into a discussion about the economy, contraception, or social justice concerns, often with side accusations such as, "But *you* don't care about the children that are already here!" If someone then attempts to bring the discussion back to abortion, it isn't long until it again becomes a discussion about everything except the topic at hand.

Yet the discussion must be had. So how do we do it? First you have to put peripheral discussions aside. The conversation is not about contraception. It is not about the economic concerns of those seeking the abortion. It is not about social justice concerns that plague black folk in America. The discussion about abortion must be about abortion! And its impact on women and the black community. So if you must, get in the mirror and argue the other issues out. Get all the rhetoric out of your system and then prepare to join us for a real look at abortion in America in the 21st century.

In preparation for discussion, homework is also required. There is a bevy of information that should be considered, including the numbers we have shared in this book because numbers do not lie. Several times we have mentioned that New York City is the most extreme example of abortion going out of control. In 2010, for every 1,000 black babies born alive, 1448 died in an abortion chamber.[45] In Georgia, more than 59% of abortions are performed on black women.[46] In Alabama more than 57% of the

[45] http://www.nyc.gov/html/doh/downloads/pdf/vs/2009sum.pdf

abortions are on black women.[47] In Mississippi the number jumps to more than *78%* on women of color[48] (Mississippi has only a 2.7% Latino population). No matter where you go, there is a pattern of abortions being performed on black women at three, four, and five times their rate in the population of each state. I recommend you take a look for yourself.

Look at other facts, including those about abortion itself. Contrary to the claims of the National Abortion Federation and other abortion providers, abortion is *not* among the safest medical procedure available. Abortion is a surgical procedure that has left a wake of dead and reproductively maimed women across the nation. It is also the most unregulated medical procedure in the nation—many abortionists have never been licensed to practice medicine in any state. Horror stories like Kermit Gosnell's from Philadelphia are just tips of the iceberg in the discussion of how women and children have suffered at the hands of abortionists throughout the nation. Stephen Brigham, Bertha Bugarin, James Pendergraft, Eileen Riley, Nicola Riley, Andrew Sutherland, Arturo Apolinario, Albert Dworkin, Rapin Osathanondh, Tyrone Malloy, and George Shepard are just a few of a growing list of abortionists who have killed or reproductively maimed women.

Then there are the more common complications from abortion which have to be considered. Perforated uterus, perforated bowel, pulling out the intestines, spreading venereal disease through unclean instruments, uterine scarring, and leaving parts of babies in utero are just a few of the possible side effects of abortion. Not to mention the fact that some women find it harder to get pregnant or carry to term after an abortion.

I just re-read Carol Everett's book, *The Scarlet Lady, Confessions of a Successful Abortionist.* Carol candidly discloses the deaths and maimings that had become almost routine in her facilities. She describes how physicians at area hospitals helped cover up the botched abortions and deaths, frequently disguising them as other female related health concerns. None of these abortionists had the

---

[46] http://oasis.state.ga.us/oasis/oasis/qryMCH.aspx

[47] http://www.adph.org/healthstats/assets/resabort09.pdf

[48] http://msdh.ms.gov/phs/2009/Bulletin/vr2009.pdf

woman's health interest at heart or even in mind. Most were in it for the multi-millions of dollars they reaped. Carol says she had set a goal of 600 abortions a month in order to become a millionaire. Her clinic would perform an abortion even if the woman was not pregnant! No one ever warned women not to seek the services of these butchers, not even the National Abortion Federation that visited Kermit Gosnell's clinic in 2009.

In *Won By Love*, the original Jane Roe—Norma McCorvey—testifies to how hygiene and disposal in the average abortion clinic is grossly inadequate. Clinics routinely rely on garbage disposals or incinerators to do their dirty work, although some harvest body parts and run lucrative trafficking businesses on the side. Notably, McCorvey has given her life to God and become a figurehead in the pro-life movement, trying to undo the damage she helped do. My friend, Sandra Cano, the original plaintiff in *Doe v. Bolton*, is also a pro-life activist now, which is another well-kept secret in the abortion industry. They don't want you to know that both of these ladies were coerced to bring abortion on demand to America.

In addition to the reproductive maiming that has happened across the nation, women are subjected to an increased risk of breast cancer as a result of their induced abortions. According to available information, "Seventy-two epidemiological studies have been conducted since 1957; and 80% of these studies have shown that abortion increases the risk of breast cancer independently of the effect of delaying the birth of a first child."[49]

Further information found in health care publications demonstrates an increased incidence of extreme premature birth risk for women with prior induced abortion as well as an increased risk of autism and cerebral palsy for subsequent children.[50] And, few if any, discuss or research the psychological impact, such as post-abortive stress syndrome or clinical depression, that abortion has had on women.[51] Many women develop problems with alcohol

[49] http://www.abortionbreastcancer.com/The_Link.htm

[50] Ibid.

[51] http://www.rachelsvineyard.org/PDF/Articles/Abortion%20and%20Post%20Traumatic%20Stress%20Disorder%20-%20Theresa%20.pdf

[52] http://www.abortionfacts.com/reardon/abortion_and_suicide.asp

[53] http://www.stopforcedabortions.org/forced.htm

or drug abuse, anxiety, eating disorders, sleeping disorders, sex or relationship problems. Some women even become suicidal after an abortion.[52] Another well-kept secret of the dark side of abortion is that more than 64% of women obtaining an abortion were coerced by a parent, minister, father of the child, or some other person in a trust relationship with the woman.[53]

Abortion hurts women, and every day the degree of harm is increasing. Whether the harm is inflicted through the abortionist, or the risks that come after, we may never know its extent because the statistics are not collected. Most states that have regulations regarding surgical centers are not enforcing the laws on the books when it comes to abortion chambers. We may never know the number of women that have been reproductively maimed and today want children but cannot have them because of a prior induced abortion.

We may never know the numbers of women that have died at the abortionist's hand, because the abortionist covered his/her tracks by calling the death something other than what it was – a botched abortion. We may never have an accurate count of the number of women now suffering from breast cancer (or who have died from breast cancer) because we refuse to discuss or disclose the clearly documented link between an induced abortion and breast cancer. Abortion hurts women and we must begin to talk about it.

But Planned Parenthood has propaganda videos which try to market abortion as no big deal—a quick fix to a desperate problem. One of the most chilling Planned Parenthood videos I have viewed includes a vignette of a married woman named Mary. In her segment, Mary tells us she had contraception failure that resulted in an unplanned pregnancy. Wanting us to believe she was being brave, she goes on to tell us that her lap was not big enough nor were her arms wide enough to hold a child. As she breathes a great sigh of relief after the procedure, she expresses her appreciation to Planned Parenthood and the services they provide. I cannot not help but wonder what that abortion did to her family. There was no discussion of her husband and whether his arms were wide enough or his lap big enough to hold that child.

How many families have been destroyed because the father of the child has no say in whether his child lives or dies? At a women's conference in Virginia, this was the question the cameraman posed to me. He wanted to know if we ever talked about, or even thought about, the harm that is done to the man who wants his child but cannot stop the mother from aborting. Then there is the shame that is keeping millions of women in the bondage of guilt from having an abortion. While attending the 2012 African Methodist Episcopal church conference in Nashville, I had the opportunity to distribute hundreds of copies of *Maafa21* to attendees. During a lull in the action at our booth, I took several packets and began to walk the venue. I stopped at a table where several black women were standing and began to share. As I did, one of the women silently cried. I knew she was post abortive, so I shared with the group that I am post abortive. After gaining their commitment to watch the DVD, I left to get more packets. The young woman that was crying while I spoke literally chased me and began to share her story. She led the conversation with, "Oh the shame..." of having had multiple abortions. How long had she carried that shame, I wonder, having been unable to share the pain of it with others? I thank God for the opportunity to share the forgiving grace of Jesus with her.

Abortion hurts women, abortion hurts families. There is no measurable way to determine the extent of the damage that has been done. Abortion also hurts communities, driving wedges between black and white, rich and poor. No matter which way the abortion coin is tossed, there is a trail of physical and emotional pain in its wake.

Across the nation, the hearts of individuals have hardened towards children so that even though abortion is murder, it is no longer abhorrent. It is seen as a tool of convenience, to prevent a *person* who is unwanted from coming and ruining our own lives. And it has become the preferred contraceptive method of family planning advocates. It doesn't elevate women—it alienates them from their own bodies. More and more women have overridden their hormonal cravings and natural urges for children, for the death of those their natural bodies craved. This is the tragedy we must end.

Action Steps

1. **Encourage** post abortive women that have been hurt by abortion to share their experience by signing the Declaration provided by Operationoutcry.org

2. **Examine** your state laws regarding ambulatory surgical centers. Are they being enforced at abortion clinics?

3. **Urge** your lawmakers to enforce the ambulatory surgical center laws if they are not being enforced

4. **Pray** for God to end the scourge of abortion in America

Chapter 15: The Targeting Must End

Recently, *USA Today* featured an article: "Black Population Falls in Major Cities."[54] Using the recently released 2010 census data, the article pointed to a host of reasons for the decline. What the article failed to include as a discussion point was the impact abortion has had on the decline in the black population across America. All but seven states have experienced some decline in the black population. Only four of the seven saw some degree of increase. These are all matters that we must set aside political doctrine to discuss, since the facts reveal we are indeed into depopulation - black genocide.

This chapter is the most difficult to write because so many people, black and white do not believe targeting is occurring. You have read in these pages of the eugenics agenda. You have read about Margaret Sanger's Negro Project. By now, I hope many of you have obtained a copy of *Maafa 21* and watched each and every minute of the story it tells. Despite these pieces of information, some of you remain skeptical about whether the abortion industry is deliberately discriminating against blacks, mostly because of your belief that the woman is *choosing* to terminate the life her child. No one is holding a gun to her head and making her abort, so many of you say.

They are not, but our law system acknowledges and punishes coercive behavior every day which is much less dramatic than a gun being held to the head. The question is not whether a black woman getting an abortion has control over her arms and faculties when she walks into an abortion clinic, but what is getting her there in the first place? Is she walking in on her own volition? Or is someone driving her into the abortion den for her own good? If evidence exists to that her own free choice would have been otherwise—to keep her baby—then there is good grounds to

[54]http://www.usatoday.com/news/nation/census/2011-03-22-1Ablacks22_ST_N.htm

believe she is being pressured. And if evidence shows a disproportionate number of black women all over the nation are making the same decision, who also would have chosen differently otherwise, there is reason to suspect targeting.

As a seasoned human resources professional, I cannot help but compare abortion through the lenses of proof required to show discrimination in the workplace. When I do, I come away convinced that discrimination against blacks in America is alive and well through abortion. I ask that you bear with me as I walk you through just a few of the actions of abortionists that support my belief they are targeting and discriminating against blacks.

As we begin this analysis, let's establish a few common elements by which we will govern our analysis:

1. In the employment arena, the person making the allegation of discrimination has the burden of proving there is intent to discriminate.

2. Usually complainants compare their treatment to the treatment of others in the workplace.

3. If there truly was discriminatory action, it has to correspond with whatever happened to the employee—be the causal force of the complaint.

4. The motive behind the person doing the discrimination has to be understood as racial in nature.

5. Any other reason, or excuse, for the discrimination can be shown to be lies.

6. Any documentation supporting the contentions being made should be examined.

Using these few steps, allow me to make my case that the abortion industry has systematically and routinely targeted the black community, thereby discriminating against them. And yes, I understand the burden is mine to make the case.

The most frequently cited example of targeting behavior by abortion clinics is the location of abortion facilities. In the early days of the birth control movement, there were many blacks who objected to birth control facilities located in urban areas where they lived. The cry over locations was actually so great that three professors in 1974 completed a study to determine if race was indeed a factor. In their study, *Family Planning Services and the Distribution of Black Americans*, authors Kenneth C. W. Kammeyer, Norman R. Yetman, and McKee J. McClendon concluded: "We only know that in most regions of the country, in poor counties and rich counties, in rural and urban counties, the same pattern appears: family planning is more likely to be available if there are black Americans in the population."[55]

The results of this study did nothing to slow the placement of birth control, and later, abortion facilities in urban areas.

In 2008, the Life Issues Institute did their own study to determine what, if any, impact race had on where Planned Parenthood abortion clinics are located. Each facility was analyzed for the percentage of black residents living within a 1, 3, and 5-mile radius of the clinic. These percentages were then compared to the percentage of blacks living in the entire city. This would determine if the facility had been placed in a more predominantly black neighborhood. In addition, the radius and city percentages were compared to the state percentage to see if either of these was higher than the state overall. The study then concluded that 60% of the abortion facilities had surrounding black populations that were measurably higher than either the city or the state average. Significantly, 34% of the facilities had a black population more than 5 percentage points higher than the surrounding city or state.[56]

A third study, completed in 2011 by Life Dynamics out of Denton, Texas concluded: "What we now know – and have documented – is that there is not one state in the union without population control centers located in ZIP codes with higher percentages of blacks and/or Hispanics than the state's overall percentage. In fact, Hawaii is the only state that does not have facilities located in ZIP codes exceeding 125% of their overall percentage."[57]

[55] Family Planning Services and the Distribution of Black Americans Author(s): Kenneth C. W. Kammeyer, Norman R. Yetman, McKee J. McClendon Source: Social Problems, Vol. 21, No. 5 (Jun., 1974), pp. 674-690 Published by: University of California Press on behalf of the Society for the Study of Social Problems, page 688

[56] http://www.protectingblacklife.org/pdf/SE_Black_Genocide_Study.pdf

[57] http://lifenews.wpengine.netdna-cdn.com/wp-

The 2012 Protecting Black Life study narrowed the focus, and is the most compelling study of all. They concluded, using 2010 census data, that 79% of Planned Parenthood surgical abortion facilities are located within walking distance of African American or Hispanic/Latino neighborhoods.[58]

It is clear that the location of abortion clinics is in disproportionately high minority areas. But why is this remarkable? Under any other circumstance, researchers, community health professionals, and others would point to these locations as factors that destabilize the community, just as they have done for years when decrying the locations of liquor stores in urban and poor neighborhoods. Typically, researchers conclude in study after study that liquor stores indeed destabilize the community. But abortion facilities do more than *destabilize* the black community; they *depopulate* the black community. They are instruments of genocide.

Unlike the liquor store locations that many communities now ban by code from being located near schools, abortuaries are sometimes right next door to schools. This is the case with the Planned Parenthood clinic on 16th Street in Washington, D.C. Locating them as such creates a sense of normalcy around the den of death, rather than outrage or fear for the lives of future generations of blacks. The simplest of questions for me, as I compare this to abortion clinics in suburban areas, is this: if there is no racial intent in the location of the abortion dens, then why aren't the majority in white areas? Here in the state of Georgia where I live, *100%* of abortuaries are located in urban areas where blacks reside. 70% of them are in the urban counties of South Fulton and DeKalb. This evidence is damning. A county by county analysis of New York reveals similar, shocking, racial targeting.[59]

The criteria Planned Parenthood uses to justify construction or modification of their facilities is another clear indicator of racial targeting. In 2011, Virginia Beach Planned Parenthood petitioned

content/uploads/2011/08/LifeDynamicsRacialReport.pdf

[58] http://www.protectingblacklife.org/pp_targets/index.html

[59] http://nyc41percent.com/

the State Board of Health to expand their facility that was completed in 2009. In their application for a certificate of public need, they described the services that would be provided once the application was approved. They said they wanted to "...expand services to include additional diagnostic and therapeutic gynecologic procedures and surgical services needed to better serve the center's patients and the community. These surgical services are a natural extension of the center's existing services and will improve access for women with little or no health coverage."[60]

Or course the new "surgical services" they wanted underinsured women to have "access" to were abortions. In describing the services the center provides, the only surgical procedure listed was "first trimester medical and aspiration pregnancy termination."[61] And in a particularly sick twist of logic, Planned Parenthood justified their need for a third surgical room because the black infant mortality rate in Virginia was ranked in the bottom half of the nation. In other words, because black babies were faring so badly once they were born, they would be better off being aborted. Virginia Beach apparently thought that giving poor black moms better "access" to "surgical facilities" would lower their infant mortality rate. Hmmm... exchanging unintentional death for murder is a good trade?

Virginia Planned Parenthood projected they would see 1800 new patients in the first year with a minimum of 3600 pre-operative visits and "surgery." In other words, a third surgical room needed to be built for a lot more black babies' deaths there. They are going to end up in the same situation that New York City is in, where the number of black abortions outnumbers the number of live births. For more than ten years, it has been that way. In any community where 60% of pregnancies end in abortion, it can only be called what it is – genocide.

---

[60] Application for a Medical Care Facilities Certificate of Public Need (Chapter 4, Article 1:1 of Title 32,1, Section 1-102.1 through 32.1-102.12 of the Code of Virginia of 1958, As Amended), page 11
[61] Ibid, page 20.

Action Steps

1. **Talk** about abortion's impact on women of color

2. **Examine** the location of abortion centers in your state. Are they in urban areas where blacks reside? Talk about it.

3. **Urge** blacks and whites in your sphere of influence to look at whether the black community is being targeted. Encourage them to speak up about it.

4. **Pray** for God to end the scourge of abortion in America.

Conclusion

I know it has been a long road through this book, with stories and statistics you've never heard before. You may even feel defensive about abortion, like it can't be that bad and I must be deceiving you somehow. But the truth will set you free.

The facts are simple. In the early 1900s, Margaret Sanger founded Planned Parenthood, not to provide free mammograms and the Pill, but to start the extinction the poor and black communities even faster than she thought evolution would. She was an admitted racist and believed birth control and abortion were the next modern tools to ensure the less desirables did not out-reproduce the more desirable.

Her successor, Allen Guttmacher, was no different. He was also a leading eugenicist and hoped to control population in urban black areas. The only difference was, he knew abortion would be a better tool than birth control to accomplish this, and therefore he expanded the reasons for abortion to include emotional concerns rather than just physical ones. This greatly increased the number of abortions—which was the intent—and generally set America on a new moral calculus which devalued life. All other factors—feelings of convenience, economics, or insecurity—were reason enough to abort a child.

The 70s legalized abortion and provided all kinds of supplementary reasons why it was actually a tool of progress, not social planning: it was sexually liberating, personally freeing, and financially uplifting; it would heal the earth, liberate underpriviliged groups, and cure poverty. But none of these promises materialized. What *did* materialize was depopulation of the black community, the original intent. We've been riding this train now for 40 years and it's safe to say that even if all its defenders today are not committed to eugenics like its founders were, they are certainly still doing their bidding.

It's not just incidental. The abortion movement has never repented of its racist origins or logic. In fact, they're still approving of it, as long as the argument is formulated in progressive liberal terms which sound magnanimous and compassionate to society as a whole. Rather than using the old eugenicist lingo which was overtly racist, they sneak it in the back door as they justify their beliefs that black urban centers should decimate their children. They hold the abortionist's knife in one hand, blood dripping down, while they hold a Martin Luther King Jr. sign in the other. They believe they are doing the black community good by mowing down its innocent, unborn lives.

But Martin Luther King prayed that someday his *children* would see change in America. He had a dream based on life. Let us pray God will end the scourge of abortion in this nation. Let's humble ourselves and repent for this country. Let's bring this nation back to our Biblical roots where life is sacred. And let's not give up until we finally tear down this last bastion of discrimination in the land of the free and home of the brave.

Action Steps

1. **Practice** your pro-life language until it naturally rolls off your tongue without thought.

2. **Role** play with other pro-life activists until your message resounds

3. **Research** the anti-life organizations in your area. What is their message against life?

4. **Pray** for the end of the scourge of abortion in America.

Appendix A: Abortion Timeline:

- 1860s: Evolutionary theory quickly becomes eugenics, or evolution applied to society

- 1900s: Margaret Sanger starts Negro Project, wealthy foundations back eugenics.

- 1907- compulsory sterilization programs begin

- 1914: Planned Parenthood begins under Sanger and Birth Control League

- 1960s: new PP director, Guttmacher expands definition of abortion to include mental health of a pregnant woman

- 1960s: feminism/sexual revolution

- 1965- anti-birth control laws struck down by Supreme Court

- 1970s: overpopulation scare sanctions abortion as population control and poverty solution

- 1973: Roe V. Wade legalizes abortion federally; Doe V. Bolton includes mental health definition and legalizes abortion throughout all nine months of pregnancy

- 1984: First Sanctity of Life Sunday, celebrating pro-life across churches nationally

- 2012: National Healthcare Act expands abortion and makes it taxpayer funded, even for Catholic/Christian institutions

Appendix B: A Proclamation

"The values and freedoms we cherish as Americans rest on our fundamental commitment to the sanctity of human life. The first of the ``unalienable rights" affirmed by our Declaration of Independence is the right to life itself, a right the Declaration states has been endowed by our Creator on all human beings -- whether young or old, weak or strong, healthy or handicapped.

Since 1973, however, more than 15 million unborn children have died in legalized abortions -- a tragedy of stunning dimensions that stands in sad contrast to our belief that each life is sacred. These children, over tenfold the number of Americans lost in all our Nation's wars, will never laugh, never sing, never experience the joy of human love; nor will they strive to heal the sick, or feed the poor, or make peace among nations. Abortion has denied them the first and most basic of human rights, and we are infinitely poorer for their loss.

We are poorer not simply for lives not led and for contributions not made, but also for the erosion of our sense of the worth and dignity of every individual. To diminish the value of one category of human life is to diminish us all. Slavery, which treated Blacks as something less than human, to be bought and sold if convenient, cheapened human life and mocked our dedication to the freedom and equality of all men and women. Can we say that abortion -- which treats the unborn as something less than human, to be destroyed if convenient -- will be less corrosive to the values we hold dear?

We have been given the precious gift of human life, made more precious still by our births in or pilgrimages to a land of freedom. It is fitting, then, on the anniversary of the Supreme Court decision in Roe v. Wade that struck down State anti-abortion laws, that we reflect anew on these blessings, and on our corresponding responsibility to guard with care the lives and freedoms of even the weakest of our fellow human beings.

Now, Therefore, I, Ronald Reagan, President of the United States of America, do hereby proclaim Sunday, January 22, 1984, as National Sanctity of Human Life Day. I call upon the citizens of this blessed land to gather on that day in homes and places of worship to give thanks for the gift of life, and to reaffirm our commitment to the dignity of every human being and the sanctity of each human life.

In Witness Whereof, I have hereunto set my hand this 13th day of January, in the year of our Lord nineteen hundred and eighty-four, and of the Independence of the United States of America the two hundred and eighth."

-Ronald Reagan

[Filed with the Office of the Federal Register, Jan. 16, 1984]

Ronald Reagan saw the connection between pro-life and civil rights, even in 1984, and was willing to speak out. As soon as people heard their conscience voiced in common sense terms, they were willing to defend their "less progressive" beliefs. Many were more willing to work as activists too.

As a result, the pro-life cause has gained a lot of ground. Culturally, the average person is more likely to say abortion is a bad thing than a good thing, at least for them personally. Every day new science and technology reveal that the unborn baby is a living, functioning being, at younger ages, and capable of experiencing sensations and even emotions.

Sanctity of Life Sunday is now practiced in churches across the country, nationally. The Church is the best hope for mounting a strong grassroots force for life. You can help by getting involved in the kinds of activities usually focused on, on Sanctity of Life Sunday: pregnancy care outreach, baby bottle funds, walks for life, pregnancy/maternal homes, canned goods and clothes for new mothers, etc. Consider supporting CareNet, Bethany Adoptive services, or any number of Christian groups started on behalf of unplanned/unwanted children.

CPSIA information can be obtained at www.ICGtesting.com
Printed in the USA
LVOW06s1433060514

384630LV00001B/250/P